THE BEST BOOK
OF
GIRLS BEHAVING
BADLY...

EVER!

ISBN 1 85868 735 7

Project Editor: Lucian Randall
Editing: Graeme Kidd and Sally Newman
Senior Art Editor: Diane Spender
Designer: Mary Ryan
Production: Garry Lewis

Printed and bound in Great Britain

THE BEST BOOK
OF
GIRLS BEHAVING
BADLY...
EVER!

Adèle Lang

CARLTON

Adèle Lang is the author of *How to Spot A Bastard by His Star Sign* and *What Katya Did Next*. She is also astrologer-with-attitude at Minx magazine, journalist-at-large for various other publications and copywriter-for-hire in the advertising world. She has little time to behave badly.

Also by Adèle Lang:
How to Spot a Bastard by his Star Sign
What Katya Did Next

To all the badly behaved good girls, past and present,
from Clinic.
You know who you are.

"Show me a woman who doesn't feel guilt and I'll show you a man."
Erica Jong

CONTENTS

1

MYTHS, LEGENDS & FAIRY TALES

1.1 WHY, WHY, WHY, DELILAH?

"Give a woman an inch and she thinks she's a ruler."
Anon

When I was very young, my mother used to tell me that little boys were made of slugs and snails and puppy dogs' tails. Little girls, on the other hand, were made of sugar and spice and all things nice. A comforting thought this when I was secretly trying to sell my Barbie*, naked, shorn and trussed, to the highest bidding six-year old schoolboy keen on owning his first ever sex object. Why do girls behave badly? Probably for the same reason as men do – because we *can*.

That isn't to say we do it only out of greed, vanity, thoughtlessness, selfishness or sheer bloody-mindedness. Girls also behave badly when wronged. Hell hath no fury like a little girl who discovers that Barbie's hair doesn't grow back when cut. And hell hath no less fury than when that same little girl is duped out of the money for her cropped and trussed doll because the delinquent buyers could outrun her.

Of course, being a badly-behaved female does have its advantages over being a badly-behaved male. We're better than boys at schools. We outnumber men as graduates. We get arrested less and spend less time in prison. In other words, we're all-round smarter than boys. Which means if we do choose to behave badly, we're cunning enough not to get found out or punished. This may explain why history books lack so many bad-girl role models. And why this little girl got her own back on all those little boys by telling the teacher that not only had they stolen her Barbie but they'd also taken its clothes off, tied it up and chopped off its beautiful long blonde hair.

*Sorry. I lied about this book containing no puerile blonde jokes.

Suicide

- Killing yourself before someone kills you.
- Killing yourself to stop you killing someone else.
- Killing yourself with an asp.

Murder

- Eating meat.
- Threatening to strangle a service-station attendant for short-changing you.
- Poisoning your partner rather than filing for divorce.

Handy Hint

Blood stains in carpet can be easily removed with a mixture of starch and water.

EVE WAS A COMFORT EATER

A Brief And Inaccurate History In Time

Apparently the past actions of girls – particularly bad girls – have helped to shape the world as we know it today. Not that you'd be able to tell this, of course, if your reading has been limited to scholarly texts such as history books. While Snow White's step-mum, Cinderella's sisters and Hansel and Gretel's witch get all the good roles in fairy tales, they don't seem to have many peers in the real world. Indeed, one of the main reasons the following period piece is so startlingly brief is that it is amazingly difficult to find anything but the sketchiest details about famous, non-fictional *femme fatales*. Often, they don't even rate a mention – which is why, on occasion, I have had to rely upon myths, legends and a certain amount of fertile, febrile imagination.

A long, long time ago

Eve Released all evil into the world by sleeping with Adam and bearing him sons. Apparently she also ate an apple, though probably only because chocolate hadn't been invented.

Pandora Released all evil into the world by opening a box, thus serving as a diabolical warning to all women tempted to rifle through their partner's pockets, wallets and briefcases.

Medusa A permanent bad hair day caused her to devour men instead of begging them for reassurance like normal women do. Perseus slew her by showing her her own reflection in his polished shield, though these days he'd be more likely to just drop her for a girl with a short, neat bob.

Sphinx Legendary female monster who asked travellers very tricky riddles (*eg Why do only women get cellulite?*), then ate them when

Not such a long time ago

Queen Victoria (1819-1901) Queen of Great Britain whose stern moral values made the lives of all married women a misery as they were forced to hide their lovers underneath beds and inside wardrobes.

Emmeline Pankhurst (1858-1928) Leader of the Suffragettes who fought for women's rights to vote, to own property and to get a good education. Then had to go and spoil it all by joining the Conservative Party.

Rosa Luxemburg (1871-1919) Misguided Polish revolutionary who was shot for espousing the glories of socialism (a political belief which deems that every girl is entitled to the same pair of badly-made shoes).

Lillie Langtry (1853-1929) First girl in Britain to prove that you didn't have to be a wanton hussy in order to be an actor – you just had to act like one.

Mata Hari (1876-1917) Exotic dancer and spy who prejudiced French national security (and questioned its manhood) by also shagging top intelligence brass from Germany.

Mrs Simpson (1896-1986) Twice-divorced American who managed to rule a king. After his abdication and their subsequent marriage, she – rather belatedly perhaps – developed a taste for very expensive jewels.

Marlene Dietrich (1901-1992) German actor who caused a massive scandal by looking a lot better in trousers than men did.

Eva Braun (1910-45) Woman with the worst taste in men in the entire history of the Universe. Ever.

Christine Keeler (1942-) Like Mata Hari except as played by Joanne Whalley-Kilmer.

Eva "Evita" Peron (1919-1952) Usual story about a young blonde marrying a well-connected bloke and immediately becoming more famous and more popular than him. Only real sin: inspiring Andrew Lloyd Webber to drag out his piano again.

Benazir Bhutto (1953-) Prime minister of Pakistan who was dismissed by the president in 1990 for corruption and incompetence but fought her way back to power again, no doubt by pointing out that politicians are expected to behave badly – even female ones.

Nancy Reagan (1923-) Reputedly the real power in the Reagan household. Allegedly employed an astrologer to help predict government policies because it was a lot more reliable than asking her husband.

Margaret Thatcher (1925-) Longest-serving Premier in twentieth century Britain and most reviled woman in history. Maybe

Monica Lewinsky (1973-) White House intern whose affair with Bill Clinton caused the biggest scandal in America since his previous one.

Gratuitous Bloke Joke

Why did God create man? Because vibrators can't buy you a drink.

1.2 NO MUSE IS EVER A GOOD MUSE

"If you obey all the rules, you miss all the fun."
Katherine Hepburn

Bad girls get admirers. Bad girls inspire men. Even good girls look up to bad girls. After all, who wants to see Maria von Trapp try to save the family unit when they can watch Glenn Close's character in *Fatal Attraction*, try to kill it instead? Who wants to sing along with Tammy Wynette to the soothing sounds of "Stand By Your Man" when they can scream at their boyfriends to the strains of Alanis Morissette? And who on earth would want to read *The Rules* when there are so many better books written by women who encourage you to break them.

Wicked Thought
Bad girls in Hollywood prefer to play good girls because it means they have less lines to rehearse.

SHOOTING THE MALE LEAD

The Top 10 Bad Girls On Film

1. Fatal Attraction

Any girl who can make out with Michael Douglas over the kitchen sink without feeling the urge to do the washing up has to be a perfect psycho. Indeed, Glenn Close's character managed to do more harm to male perceptions of unmarried career girls than Bridget Jones or Ally McBeal could ever hope to do. To even the score a little, director Adrian Lyne did try to ensure that Anne Archer's character did just as much damage to the image of frigid and servile housewives.

2. Basic Instinct

Any girl who can make out with Michael Douglas, anywhere and at any time, should be allowed as many ice-picks under her pillow as she wants. And any man who claims he can make out what's between Sharon Stone's legs when she crosses them down at the police station, must have an extremely good imagination.

3. Disclosure

Any girl who can make out with Michael Douglas over an office desk without feeling the urge to slit her wrists with a nearby letter opener, should at least be allowed to sue him for sexual harassment afterwards. And get damages for appearing in a film with one of the most laughable, unbelievable plotlines in the history of cinema.

4. The Last Seduction

Probably the only American film ever whose bad girl character doesn't blame her vile behaviour on a neglected childhood, a poor education or lack of sex. Nor does she redeem herself by being killed by any of her co-stars at the end. Amoral bitch Bridget, as played in an Oscar-worth performance by Linda Fiorentino, is the only woman in this list that men should be afraid of. Very afraid of indeed.

5. Gone With The Wind

Brilliant as Scarlett O'Hara, Vivienne Leigh manages to turn the arche-typal, simpering Southern belle into a manipulative, willful and petulant little minx, thus teaching female viewers all over the world that a girl doesn't have to be a Stepford Wife like Melanie in order to get what she wants from a man.

6. Misery

Taking a misogynistic male author hostage and breaking his legs in several places with a heavy implement when he refuses to make his female character more sympathetic is absolutely not on – unless the author's name is Stephen King, of course.

7. Betty Blue

From having hot sex with a Frenchman to burning a house down and then deciding to stab a rude man with a fork, Beatrice Dalle's charac-ter had bad girls everywhere rooting for her and wishing they were brave enough to be as uninhibited themselves. Until, that is, they found out that Betty was basically stark-raving bonkers. Then they just wanted to be like her even more.

8. Thelma & Louise

Hailed as an action movie for girls, this good-guys-on-the-run-from-bad-guys had only one thing that made it completely different from movies starring Bruce Willis, Sylvester Stallone or Harrison Ford: the heroes, Geena Davis and Susan Sarandon, die in the end.

9. Frances

Based on the tragic real-life story of the talented actor Frances Farmer, the equally as talented Jessica Lange portrays how a rebellious woman with a big mouth was silenced intermittently by an over-ambitious mother, a ruthless Hollywood system and a negligent mental institution. A frightening moral tale that just goes to show that while good girls go on to win Oscars, bad girls stay back for electrotherapy.

10. The Exorcist

Linda Blair's star turn as cute-little-tyke-possessed-by-the-devil had real-life mothers looking sideways at their pre-pubescent daughters every time the kids started to look severely disturbed – no doubt after having had to watch such an evil film.

Other women to watch

- Bette Midler's captive audience in *Ruthless People*.
- Bette Davis' spiteful sister act in *What Ever Happened to Baby Jane?*
- Darryl Hannah's lethal acrobatic skills in *Blade Runner*.
- Faye Dunaway's cheekbones in *Bonnie and Clyde*.
- Laura San Giacomo's sibling rivalry in *Sex, Lies and Videotape*.
- Kathleen Turner's murderous wife in *Body Heat*.

- Kathleen Turner's murderous wife in *War of The Roses*.
- Sandra Bernhard's frightening little rich girl in *King of Comedy*.
- Sean Young's back-seat driving in *No Way Out*.
- Stockard Channing's bad student in *Grease*.
- Ellin Barkin's single mother skills in *Sea of Love*.
- Kim Basinger's housekeeping skills in *9 1/2 Weeks*.
- Sigourney Weaver's bitch-in-suit in *Working Girl*.
- Theresa Russell's bad relationship techniques in *Black Widow*.
- Christina Ricci's callous cow-act in *The Opposite of Sex*.
- Drew Barrymore's venomous vamp-act in *Poison Ivy*.
- Juliette Binoche's head-banging antics in *Damage*.
- Jennifer Jason Leigh in anything.

Honorable mentions on the small screen

Roseanne in *Roseanne*.

Edina and Patsy in *Absolutely Fabulous*.

Sybil in *Fawlty Towers*.

Kristin in *Dallas*.

Alexis in *Dynasty*.

Amanda and Sydney in *Melrose Place*.

Shannon in *Beverly Hills 90210*.

Elaine in *Seinfeld*.

Queenie in *Black Adder*.

Mrs Merton.

Viewer's Guide

*Unless you want to lose your lunch, try to avoid watching any
film starring Julie Andrews, Sally Fields or Meg Ryan.*

SEX AND DRUGS AND A PACKET OF TAMPAX

Bad Girls In Rock

Tori Amos Inspired a new generation of young mums to opt for the benefits of bottle-feeding, simply by posing topless on a record cover, suckling a piglet.

Josephine Baker Black singer and dancer who entertained Parisiennes in the Twenties and proved to her critics that just because a girl takes her clothes off doesn't mean she can't also adopt starving children, risk her life for the French Resistance and win a medal for her efforts.

Maria Callas Beautiful opera singer who slept with Greek tycoon Aristotle Onassis. Her other repulsive act was to allegedly have had a tapeworm surgically placed in her intestine in order to stay thin.

Belinda Carlisle Ex-lead vocalist from The Go-Gos who is living proof that, so long as you've got good bones, you can go on as many binges as you like and still not lose your looks.

Bjork Icelandic singer who achieved international acclaim and gained an entire new legion of fans when she beat up a journalist at Bangkok airport.

Mariah Carey Has shown that girls too can walk out on their lesser-known spouse when they get really famous.

Cher Has given hope to women the world over who previously thought that if they wore leather g-strings in public over the age of 40, or sang "Believe" over the age of 50, they'd be run out of town.

Celine Dion Has proved once and for all that Barbra Streisand isn't the only female singing star who can conquer the world without having to rely on her looks.

Marianne Faithfull Sixties casualty and Eighties come-back who serves as a warning to wannabe stars that Mars Bars aren't good for your image, and neither is Mick Jagger.

Judy Garland Child star and singer *par excellence* who proved that, when they're not listening to Village People, gay men really do have the best taste in music.

Deborah Harry Blonde vixen and vocalist who, in her heyday, managed to make dark roots look attractive and bin-liners seem like a viable option on a Friday night, if Oxfam was closed.

PJ Harvey Britain's angst-ridden answer to Liz Phair and proof that the more talented you are the less your records will sell.

Billy Holiday Black jazz singer who had an extremely hard life, made easier only with the help of hard drugs.

Whitney Houston Rich, slim, gorgeous and gifted singer who, by marrying Bobby Brown, proved you can't have it all.

Chrissie Hynde Lead singer of The Pretenders, most famous for outliving many of her band members and certainly out-shining her ex-husbands (where art thou now, Ray Davies and Jim Kerr?).

Janet Jackson Inspires admiration for two reasons: 1. Her ability to cope with embarrassing family members; 2. Her ability to continue to sing despite the fact that she can't.

Wendy James Ex-lead singer of British band Transvision Vamp whose unnaturally-blonde good looks and flagrant self-promotion obscured what she actually did best: sing.

Grace Jones Darkly handsome diva of the dance floor with infinite capacity for baring breasts and/or teeth. Gained a lot of admirers by whacking the odd television presenter now and again.

Janis Joplin Blues singer who rates up there with the bad boys of rock when it comes to living hard, dying young and leaving a fairly bloated corpse.

Courtney Love A recent Hollywood makeover proves she scrubs up well when she wants to, though the occasional comforting slip-up reveals that the bad girl may be screaming to be let out again.

Madonna Having undergone more transformations than the Volkswagen Beetle, Madonna Ciccone proves once and for all that you can't keep a bad girl down, even after that godawful *Sex* book.

Cerys Matthews Lead singer of Welsh band Catatonia. Like her more famous male peers Tom Jones and Richard Burton, she can sing her butt off and likes the occasional drink. Unlike either of them though, she's still got the youth and vigour to carry it off.

Liza Minnelli Daughter of Judy Garland. Carried the torch passed on by her mother by proving that, when they're not listening to The Pet Shop Boys, gay men really do have the best taste in music.

Alanis Morissette Canadian who probably caused more girls to give more men a hard time since PMT was invented.

Stevie Nicks One-time singer for Fleetwood Mac, she set the trend for entering rehab and getting famous all over again because of it.

Sinead O'Connor Irish chanteuse who gives tribute albums and their listeners a piece of her heart, and who once tried to give the Pope a piece of her mind.

Yoko Ono Supercool caterwauler accused of breaking up The Beatles (no bad thing, really, even if she didn't actually do it).

Liz Phair America's angst-ridden answer to PJ Harvey and proof that the more talented you are the less your records will sell.

Siouxsie Sioux Lead singer of The Banshees. Often bared her breasts to show that punk girls can be lady-like too and once had a tiff with a television presenter which indirectly inspired those brave boys the Sex Pistols to say the 'F' word live on air. Ooo-er.

Tina Turner The grandmother of rock who's far more appealing to look at or listen to than all those grandfathers of rock.

Written in Stone

If you want to look young and gorgeous, why not try dating a Rolling Stone?

THROWING THE BOOK AT HER

Bad Girls In Print

Jane Austen Extremely chaste, well-behaved writer who wreaked her revenge on the rest of us more worldly, less bookish types by making us sit through all her TV and film adaptations.

Julie Burchill Archetypal bad girl, journalist, columnist and author whose rather colourful love-life tends to pervade her public prose – and sometimes even manages to outshine it.

Barbara Cartland The only person alive who takes the quaint old concept of virgins and exploits it more than Richard Branson.

Jackie Collins Queen of the bonk-buster and more literary sister of Joan. Sells most of her books to intelligent readers who can't find Anton Chekov in the airport bookshop.

Helen Fielding Columnist and author of *The Diary of Bridget Jones*, the late-nineties phenomenon that shattered the myth of the strong, got-it-all-together single girl and showed us all up for the completely pathetic, weak-at-the-knees creatures we are.

Germaine Greer Australian feminist writer whose ground-breaking, best-selling book *The Female Eunuch* has probably now been outsold by *The Diary of Bridget Jones*.

Erica Jong After *Fear of Flying*, the "zippedless fuck" entered common parlance. And then left again.

Anais Nin Writer who managed to make smut seem intellectual by dint of being born in France.

Camille Paglia Controversial feminist who seem to think Madonna is a feminist icon and that date-rape wouldn't exist if girls just said "no".

Dorothy Parker More famous for her vitriolic verbal assaults than for anything she actually wrote.

Sylvia Plath Brilliant but doomed American poet and author who serves as muse-in-a-bell-jar to every depressed teenage girl the world over. Married Ted Hughes, another famous poet (though most girls would be hard-pressed to remember any of *his* poems).

Danielle Steele Queen of pap whose own life is a lot more interesting than her fiction. Has married at least a billion times (once to a convicted rapist) so should know better than to foist happy-ever-afters on to the rest of us.

Elizabeth Wurtzel Incurred the wrath of the two-aspirin-and-a-goodnight's-sleep brigade by writing the autobiographical *Prozac Nation*. Incurred the wrath of writers by starring on all her own book covers looking very attractive, intelligent and young.

Reader Advice

Save money on buying books by sitting next to other people on the train and reading their books over their shoulders.

1.3 SAINT, SINNER OR TWO-FACED COW?

"The wicked do well in this world and saints do well in the next."
Anon

Sin is the flip-side of saintliness. It's burning the steak instead of being burnt at it. It's eating stray dogs rather than feeding them. It's refusing to help third-world children and getting them to run up a decent, cheap pair of jeans instead.

Whereas good girls get canonized, bad ones get shot at. But what the hell. Unless you get regular visitations from God or you actually enjoy mingling with lepers, you're far more likely to get worshipped and idolized if you act like a complete cow.

Stating the Obvious
Bad girls will never be compared to Joan of Arc, Doris Day, Audrey Hepburn, Martha Stewart, Shirley Temple or to Mother Teresa.

OUT OF EVERYTHING BAD COMES SOMETHING WORSE

Making A Virtue Out Of The Seven Deadly Sins

It must be said that, until perusing Catholic Corner on the Internet, I actually thought The Seven Deadly Sins, according to the gospel of anyone male, were:

1. *Shopping.*

2. *Smoking.*

3. *Getting drunk.*

4. *Getting fat.*

5. *Looking old.*

6. *Holding an opinion.*

7. *Asking for a commitment.*

Of course, after perusing Catholic Corner, I came to the conclusion that the original Seven Deadly Sins must have been devised by some mealy-mouthed man who couldn't stand the thought of girls having fun without him or in spite of him.

Pride

The unerring belief that the earth would stop rotating on its axis if you left the room momentarily, Pride is much better than the opposite virtue Humility – in a bad girl, meek-like behaviour looks far too much like false modesty.

Ways to act with pride
- Refuse to wear anything comfortable just for the sake of it.
- Refuse to go anywhere without concealer, foundation or a large pair of sunglasses.
- Refuse to open a letter if the sender has spelt your name wrong on the front of it.

Greed

Greed is good providing you've got the means to feed it. Rich parents, besotted boyfriends, gullible bosses, desperate bank managers, unlimited credit cards, autumn catalogues and summer sales all do the job very nicely.

Ways to appear greedy
- Ask for a pay rise.
- Ask for a discount.
- Ask for your free make-up bag with mini-mascara that runs out after the fourth eyelash, little lipstick that's not your colour, and complexion-enhancer that doesn't suit your skin type.

Lust

Impure thoughts are the bane of a bad girl's existence – mainly because they stop her from pursuing more worthy causes like sustaining relationships, keeping jobs or saving tuna from dolphin-friendly fishing nets.

Ways to be lustful

- Invite your cab driver up for a nightcap – even when you aren't drunk.
- Loathe a man's character but sleep with him anyway.
- Complain to a male colleague about sex discrimination in the workplace while at the same time, mentally undressing him.

Anger

An overwhelming desire for revenge never makes a girl look attractive, especially if she's also wearing blue mascara. However, if you must start venting your spleen or rupturing someone else's, always remember to do it in a public place.

Ways to get angry

- Ask a palely-loitering, languishing-out-of-work-actor for an ashtray.
- Ask him for the menu and then refuse to order anything from the specials list because he took so long to recite it.
- Refuse to tip him because he took so long bringing the bill, and then torch the restaurant while he's still in it.

Gluttony

The tendency to eat like a pig, drink like a fish and smoke like a herring isn't limited to bulimic alcoholics with a 60-cigarettes-a-day habit. Even girls who *aren't* professional models are sometimes guilty of indulging too much.

Ways to overdo it

- Eat an entire packet of Chocolate Hobnobs without pausing to consider the fact that the wrapping may contain calories.

- Leave an all-you-can-eat-for-less-than-£6 Chinese restaurant with a doggy bag.
- Drink more than one bottle of paint stripper while you're decorating your house.

Covetousness

Don't be so hard on yourself for your little green monsters. It's only natural to play host to feelings of bitterness and spite when someone does better in this world than you do – particularly if they're younger and better looking as well.

Ways to feel jealous
- Find out that models aren't lying when they say they can eat anything they like.
- Find out that Nicole Kidman doesn't have a life-threatening disease.
- Find out that your similarly single girlfriend has just scored a date.

Sloth

A case of 'A' for Apathy and 'D' for Diligence, Sloth is ideal for girls who can't be bothered to behave well because it takes far too much effort.

Ways to appear sloth-like
- Ring Directory Enquiries instead of using the telephone directory.
- Throw away dirty clothes rather than washing them.
- Acquire bed sores.

Fashion Tip
To appear more virtuous, why not wear a habit?

MADONNA OR *MADONNA*?

The Quiz That Puts Your Feminine Wiles To The Test

Good cop or bad cop? Black hat or white hat? Virgin or whore? Find out what you are by taking the following, carefully-devised, psychological test. Feel free to cheat.

1. *A friend asks you what you really think of her new haircut. You:*
   a. *Silently think it makes her look like she's been dragged through an Amazon rainforest backwards, but don't have the heart to tell her.*
   b. *Tell her it's not as bad as her last one, then immediately feel bad about it and say "Just joking".*
   c. *Tell her it looks great, knowing full well you'll get all the admiring stares from men when the two of you go out together.*
   d. *Tell her she looks a fright.*

2. *Your boss tells you you've missed out on that much-desired promotion. You:*
   a. *Bow your head in deference and concede that Sister Agnes was probably the best man for the job after all.*
   b. *Hurl his cup of coffee at his head and then try to patch things up by offering to make him another one.*
   c. *Smile cheerfully at him, say "Fair enough", and then send a fax to his wife detailing the affair he's been having with that slag from accounts.*
   d. *Beat up the girl who answered 'c' to this question for attempting to spoil your office romance.*

3. *Your mother calls and asks you if it's true what they say about you in the papers. You reply:*

a. *"What? About my pending sainthood? Oh, that silly old thing."*

b. *"No, but can you lie?"*

c. *"Yes, but can you lie?"*

d. *"Which one?"*

4. *A long-lost lover arrives unexpectedly on your doorstep. Do you:*

a. *Tell him to be gone, for you are no longer a creature of earthly desires.*

b. *Knee him in the bollocks for deserting you, then let him in.*

c. *Let him in, then knee him in the bollocks.*

d. *Order two pints of half-skimmed, one pot of cream and ask him to cough up his outstanding child-maintenance payments.*

5. *You are asked to baby-sit a friend's child for an evening. Your immediate instinct is to:*

a. *Wonder how Mother Superior managed to make it this far with an illegitimate child, but agree to mind the latter all the same.*

b. *Twist your face, scuffle your feet, grunt and say "Yes, of course, I'd love to."*

c. *Nod and beam brightly while secretly regretting your decision not to lend her the money for the abortion she wanted to have a couple of years back.*

d. *Ask what the going rate per hour is.*

6. *If you found a twenty-pound note in the back of a taxicab, you would:*

a. *Wonder what it was.*

b. *Surreptitiously slip it into your bag and then tip the driver twenty quid afterwards because you feel so guilty.*

c. *Ostentatiously donate it to charity and then resent neglected children/beaten wives/starving elephants for the rest of your life.*

d. *Immediately give it to the driver. After all, judging by the state of his attire, he needs it more than you do.*

7. Love is:

   a. *Our Lord's way.*

   b. *Playing hard to get with a man and then having a panic attack when he doesn't return your call.*

   c. *Three pairs of Gucci shoes, two Prada handbags and a Cartier watch – but don't tell him that.*

   d. *Something you have to settle for when you're too old to have sex.*

8. Life is:

   a. *Something that passes you by while you're busy washing the church windows.*

   b. *Like a box of chocolates but you're on a diet.*

   c. *To be lived to the fullest, preferably at someone else's expense.*

   d. *A bitch and I've got her number.*

9. Your idea of psychopathic behaviour is:

   a. *Stealing from the collection plate.*

   b. *Setting fire to your ex-boyfriend's flat knowing full well that he's out at the time.*

   c. *Pulling wings off butterflies while bearing a pained "This is hurting me more than you" expression on your face.*

   d. *Wetting yourself when you read the previous three piss-poor examples of bad behaviour.*

10. A sociopath is

   a. *One of God's children.*

   b. *Someone who turns up to your lavish dinner party without bringing an equally lavish bottle of wine.*

c. Someone who openly dislikes you as much as you secretly dislike them.

d. Someone who gets on well with animals.

How did you score?

Mostly 'A's
The Novice Meek. Humble. Kind. Tolerant. You're the kind of girl who'd try the patience of saints, especially since you make them look like a bunch of politicians at a sales conference. In fact, if you get any nicer, even The Father, Son and Holy Ghost may start to feel threatened.

Mostly 'B's
The Fake Poor, poor you. A good girl who truly wants to be bad but can't actually cut it. Even if you were capable of slicing, dicing and chopping your enemies into lots of little pieces, you'd still feel the need to apologize for making a mess on their kitchen benches.

Mostly 'C's
The Liar You're worse than a bad girl. You're Mother Theresa in Gucci sandals, Mother Mary with a condom in her pocket. You're a bad girl who *pretends* to be good. Come on now. Stop the lies and reveal your true colours, you black-hearted soul.

Mostly 'D's
The Bad Girl Congratulations. You're a complete cow. And you probably don't have any need to read this book any further since you've got your own especially twisted version stashed in your top drawer (along with the silk knickers and the pearl-handled gun).

1.4 TERMS OF ENDEARMENT

"A lady is a woman who never shows her underwear unintentionally."
Lillian Day

When you're a bad girl, you get called all sorts of names and stand accused of all sorts of crimes. You wouldn't care, of course, if the mostly male culprits had an imaginative vocabulary, or if their silly little smear campaigns were actually true and didn't tend to reflect their inadequacies rather more than your own...

BETTER A BITCH THAN A BLOKE

Enlightened Definitions For The Damned

A
angel Wears white well. Bears no resemblance whatsoever to anything found on earth.

B
babe Famous pig.
baggage (Colloq. bag) Something a girl would have a lot less of if man hadn't been created.
ball-breaker Female who has achieved as much success as a male – or more.
banshee Girl who screams loudly a lot – usually with good reason.
biddy Much older female who is smarter than she acts.

bimbo Younger version of a *biddy*.

bird Creature with wings.

bitch Girl who speaks her thoughts out loud.

black widow Girl who eats men for breakfast.

bunny-boiler Girl who makes cheating husbands pay for their sins.

C

call girl A girl of unusually high intelligence.

cat Animal detested by most men.

chick Term American males use before being kneed in the nether regions.

cock-teaser Girl who demands money halfway through oral sex.

coquette Girl who flutters eyelashes at gullible men.

courtesan Like a call girl, but clients have much better pedigrees.

cow Animal that moos.

crone Extremely old woman who is wiser than her years.

D

diva Excellent female singer who knows her own worth.

drama queen Girl who makes reality a lot more exciting.

dyke Any girl who rejects a man's advances.

E

enchantress Girl who pretends to listen to a man while he's talking.

F

feminist Female who can take the rubbish out by herself.

femme fatale Girl who men would kill for.

fishwife Girl who swears when she's angry, usually for good reason.

floozy Girl who sleeps around as much as a man.

G

goddess Girl who is too good for mortal man.

gold-digger Girl who is smart enough to get a rich man.

granny Woman who can be relied upon to take the side of her daughter's daughter.

groupie Girl who prefers to sleep with a pop star rather than listen to his music.

H

hag Any girl who has forgotten to put her make-up on.

harlot See *floozy*.

harpy See *hag*.

harridan Older woman who can fend off muggers.

hellcat Girl willing to fight a male for her share of the duvet.

housewife Girl who works harder than her husband.

hussy Girl who is more popular with members of the opposite sex than most.

I

ingénue Girl who pretends to be a virgin.

it girl Girl with enviable lifestyle.

T

tart A sweet pie.

temptress Girl who can cook.

termagant Girl with hot temper.

tomboy Girl who wants a gun for Christmas.

tramp Girl who likes long walks.

trollop Girl who doesn't make her bed in the morning.

V

vamp Girl who charms men simply by breathing.

virago See *termagant*.

virgin See *nun*.

vixen A female fox.

W

whore Girl caught by her husband in *flagrante delicto*.

wildcat Girl who is better than her partner in bed.

witch Girl who flies at a man with her broomstick.

woman Girl with experience.

Did you know?

Most girls only use that four-letter "C" word when referring to a man.

TRUST A MAN TO SAY THAT

Patronizing Phrases And Condescending Clichés

She's driving me nuts I'm in love with her.

She doesn't understand me Can I sleep with you instead?

She doesn't believe in marriage She laughed when I proposed.

She doesn't want children She doesn't want mine.

She hates kids Especially mine.

She loves kids Well, she loves *me*.

She's good with animals She treats me very well.

She's too possessive She gets upset when I chat up other girls.

She left me for another bloke She left me for another bloke.

She didn't want to hurt my feelings She got married on the sly.

She's never cheated on me She's never told me that she has.

She would never cheat on me She would never tell me anyway.

She's a dark horse She won't tell me how many men she slept with in the past.

She's trouble She's brilliant in bed.

She's a complete, bloody bitch I'm still in love with her.

She's mad She shows her emotions.

She's very independent I don't want her to rely on me.

She's too independent She doesn't rely on me.

She hates all my friends She hates all my friends.

She doesn't get on with my mother I'm a mummy's boy.

She deserves a good slapping She just caught me out.

She's selfish She won't let me watch the football.

She's a spoilt little so-and-so We have to watch *Friends* instead.

She could talk the hind leg off a donkey I haven't got a thing to say for myself.

She's a good listener I talk a lot.

She's too demanding She wants sex every night.

She's a raving nympho She wants sex three times a night.

She's a raving lunatic She expects me to sleep in the wet patch.

She's an accident waiting to happen She's more exciting than me.

She's dangerous I could fall in love with her.

She eats men for breakfast Lucky bastards.

She always thinks she's in the right She is in the right.

She's scary She's good looking *and* intelligent.

She's turned my life around I don't drink so much any more.

She's changed my life She hoovered my bedroom.

She's tamed me I wouldn't dare look at another girl.

She's a saint She makes me look like a piece of shit.

She's a slut She's slept with someone other than me.

She's a real heartbreaker She's going to leave me.

She's hard work She expects me to carry the shopping bags.

She's got crap taste in music She doesn't like my CD collection.

She's got me by the balls She won't sleep with me until I marry her.

She'd give any bloke a run for his money She's all yours.

She's all yours Touch her and you're dead meat.

She's deep in denial She reckons she's not in love with me.

She's a lost cause I've realized she's not in love with me.

She's hopeless with money She's hopeless with my money.

She's one of life's givers She gives more than I give.

She's one of life's takers She takes more than I give.

She'd make a great wife I don't fancy her.

She'd make a great mother She's got big hips.

She makes me feel like a man She lets me be on top in bed.

She makes me feel inadequate She prefers to be on top in bed.

She's up for it She's smiled at me. Once.

She needs a good shagging She wouldn't touch me with a barge-pole.

She obviously didn't get a bit last night It's her fault for not fancying me.

She's a bit intense She's got a high IQ.

She's a bit full on She's more exciting than me.

She's a bit of all right I don't stand a chance.

She won't stop hassling me She won't let me get away with behaving badly.

She's frigid She doesn't like sleeping with me.

She's no oil painting She's about as attractive as I am.

She's a really good friend I haven't slept with her yet.

She's like a sister to me She won't sleep with me.

She's so up herself She's too good for me.

She's actually quite shy She talks more than me.

She's too good for me She's too good for me.

She's got a father complex I'm too young for her.

She's just like her mother She's got me under her thumb.

She's not the one She is the one but I won't know it until she delivers an ultimatum.

She's the love of my life She hasn't told me off – yet.

She's always changing her mind She's decided to leave me again.

She doesn't know her own mind She's decided to dump me.

She's too clingy She's just asked me what time I'm coming home for dinner.

She's always nagging me She's always asking me to do the right thing by her.

She expects too much She thinks I'm perfect.

She's got problems I'm determined to be one of them.

She's come undone I've just dropped her.

She needs to be protected from herself She's just threatened to kill me.

She's totally lost it She's just attempted to kill me.

She's manipulative She got off with self-defence.

She plays games She always beats me at Scrabble.

She's no fun She doesn't play games.

She stifles me She wants to have a turn on my PlayStation.

She's only after me for my money She's certainly not after me for my looks.

She's a pain in the neck I'm still in love with her.

She's one of those career-woman types She earns more money than me.

She's a great cook I'm not going to marry her.

She's such a romantic She gets cross when I leave the toilet seat up.

She has the patience of a saint She puts up with crap from me.

She's obviously having her period She yelled at me for behaving like a pig.

She's a strong woman She'll cope with any kind of crap I give her.

Did You Know?

Bullet holes in windows can be quickly and cheaply repaired using a few dabs of clear nail varnish.

2

LOVE,
HONOUR &
DISOBEDIENCE

2.1 UNDER FOUR MINUTES AND I'LL RUN A MILE

"My ultimate fantasy is to entice a man into my bedroom,
put a gun to his head, and say 'make babies or die' ."
Ruby Wax

Some men will pretend to dribble at the sight of you. Some men will pretend they don't like you at all. Some will fancy you less than themselves and some will fancy you less than their mums. Some will be attracted to you for your looks. Others will be drawn by your money. A few will desire you despite the fact that you're a girl, but more will desire you just because you are one. Smart ones will be happy to ogle you from a distance. Dumb ones will have to make do with perving at you from a nearby stretcher. And, needless to say, none of them will lust after you in the least when you tell them all they were crap in bed.

It's only fair that a bad girl like you tells a man what he's doing wrong as soon as he has done it. Otherwise you can't reach your sexual peak prematurely (and who wants to wait until they're fat, furrowed and in their 40s to feel the earth moving properly?). Of course, if the only men at your disposal are over 18 and not on Viagra, you may have to hang out at all-boys schools to accomplish your mission. Because even that one lone man who can muster up enough energy to serve up sex for breakfast, lunch and tea – and during snacks in between – is usually only capable of being an unstoppable sex machine for short periods of time. Once you're back to that grim reality called lust, after the dust settles, he'll be so ridden with back problems and so up to his groin in Deep Heat, bandages and splints, he won't be able to hold your interest for very much longer. Which is probably why you've just had him carted off on a stretcher.

Military Manoeuvre

To ensure a man doesn't lose his erection during sex, always keep your gun well out of sight throughout.

I'LL HAVE WHAT HE'S HAVING

Why The Female Of The Species Is Just As Deadly

Man-bashing has become a national pass-time. All men are bastards. All men should die. While there's a lot of fun to be had with making such sweeping statements and mass generalizations about the opposite sex, you can't go casting stones at the shambolic sty that is the boy-next-door's place before looking at your own less-than-rosy backyard first.

Besides, it takes a female to point out that her gender is far from perfect. If a man were brave enough to say it, we'd call him a sexist pig.

All men are cheating swine. Unless some mysterious lone siren is shagging around the clock for England, for all the males playing around there must an equal number of females conspiring with them. In fact, the only reason surveys show that more men are unfaithful than women is because women are not just the fairer sex, they are also the smartest. Girls keep quiet about their extra-curricular shenanigans. They are genetically less inclined to brag about their conquests. They are therefore also less likely to get found out.

All men are emotional cripples. If this is true, then how come every single one of your ex-lovers ends up with someone who claims he's the warmest, sweetest, most sensitive bloke in the entire Universe and goes on to state that you must have a heart the size of a very small marble not to have appreciated him?

All men are commitment-phobes. Research suggests married men are happier than single ones. The same research reckons single women are happier than married ones. A bundle of other research indicates that more women instigate divorce proceedings than men. Oh, and not forgetting, or course, the fact that, as opposed to their female counterparts, after a break-up most boyfriends start dating sooner and most divorced men get married quicker. So who's afraid of being tied down then?

All men like women who play hard to get. And you, naturally, only like men who act available. You prefer that teeth-grinding pain-in-the-butt who deluges you with phone calls, dinner dates and bouquets of flowers every day. Call me a been-there, done-that, got-the-self-inflicted-emotional-scars-to-prove-it know-it-all, but my bet is that the love of your life thus far is the one who consistently lets you down, always stands you up and never fails to forget your birthday.

All men are lead by their you-know-whats. And what, pray, are you led by? Why wear short skirts, high heels and make-up just so you can have a deep and meaningful over-the-coffee-machine with the stud-muffin at work? If you really wanted to encourage men to focus on your stunning personality and mind-bogglingly high IQ, you'd sidle up to them in a full-length paper bag.

All men judge women by their looks. Correction. Men and *women* judge women by their looks. How many times have you dismissed a girl as a bimbo because **a)** she's got blonder hair than you and **b)** you're jealous? How many times have you derided one of your own sex as plain and passed it because **a)** well, she is and **b)** because, well, you're not?

Men are always trying to re-live their youth by dating younger women. You, in turn, piously prefer blokes who take their teeth out at night. Unless you've got an extremely distant father complex, you too, given half the chance, salary and job promotions, would opt for a fresh-faced bit of rough.

Face it. Men are biologically conditioned to be self-serving, lovephobic shag-rats. We girls aren't. So we therefore don't have the same excuse. Nature has saddled us with depressing adjectives like "nurturing", "steadfast" and "loyal". So, if you do choose to ape men's inherently bad behaviour then don't feel bitter when he beats you hands down – it's because he's a born natural at it. You've really got no-one but yourself to blame. (And, thankfully, guilt at least is still one of a girl's good points. No matter how bad she is).

Sex Tip

Avoid a man ejaculating prematurely by having your orgasm first.

WELL...AT LEAST IT'S GOT A PULSE

A Few Men Worth Seducing Just For A Laugh

Here's where I raise a well-plucked eyebrow, let out a withering sigh, stub out my cigarette on the nearest hairy chest and point out the blatantly obvious to badly-behaved girls who claim they can't find a single man who's foolish enough to take them on.

The Eligible Bachelor Only eligible because he's inherited a cold, dank, dark, damp, crumbling pile in the country and only a bachelor because he won't do anything about the central heating.

The Toxic Divorcee Comes complete with a half-empty bank account and an unshakeable belief that all women are treacherous cows. You'd probably be inclined to agree if you stuck around long enough and if you hadn't started shagging other blokes in order to avoid his insufferable rants.

The Single Dad Worse than The Toxic Divorcee, because this one got lumbered with his ex-wife's kids. He'll continually stand you up on dates because "Toby's got a raging temperature again". And you can't even throttle the brat unless you want to look like a bitch without even trying.

The Sensitive Artist Usually ends up with a torn canvas, a very low bank account and an unerring belief that you are deliberately thwarting his creative aspirations and intercepting his royalty payments. Of course, he's absolutely right on both counts.

The School Boy A bad girl seducing a schoolboy is a bit like a ten-ton lorry bearing down on a very small mouse in over-sized boots. While your average 16-year-old isn't well-versed in the basic art of pleasuring a grown woman (ie washing, cooking, buying costly gifts) he can be frightened into learning very, very quickly.

The Unemployed Vagrant Whether he's squatting in a shoebox or pounding the pavement in his bare feet, this bloke is usually good-looking in a malnourished, out-of-work-actor kind of way. Plus he can always be relied upon for cheap help around the house and grateful sex – either that or face being thrown out on the streets again.

The Overweight Businessman He's flush with success, money and too much drinking during working hours. He's usually also vain, boring and impotent. So it's probably just as well he insists upon sex with the lights off – otherwise he'd see you were reading this book by torchlight under the bedclothes.

The Octogenarian Only ever consider him if you need an effective backdrop against which you can look even younger and more attractive than usual. And then only if you've just had a lobotomy and give the impression that it would take you the best part of a week to recite your own telephone number.

The Svengali Amateur theatrics will be turned into soap operas, and screaming blue murder will be transformed into number one hits. The Svengali likes nothing more than taking a good girl and making her better – or, more often the case, taking a bad girl and making her even worse.

The Boy Next Door *(also known as The Closet Case)* Dull, boring, with a proper nine-to-five job, The Boy Next Door is about as exciting as thrush and about as hard to get rid of. To put you off even further, he lives at home with his mother and often has a best friend named Pierre who always sniffs disapprovingly in the background on dates.

The Professional Gigolo The package preferred by most discerning career girls *d'un certain age*, mainly because he'll never answer back, he'll always perform on demand and he'll even say you look gorgeous when you know that you don't.

The Ex-Husband Every bad girl should have at least one ex-husband waiting in the wings, in case one of her new protégés fails to perform.

Of course, he only does your bidding because he thinks you might one day relent and give him his half of the house back.

Mr Wrong *(also known as The Co-Dependent)* Useful only if you have been commissioned to write your autobiography and want to double the dose of melodrama. He'll match you and your bad habits, drink for drink and tantrum for tantrum. And then when, in a dramatic attempt at role-reversal, you start nagging him until the cows come home, he will still go out and sleep with the lot of them.

Vital Statistic

Researchers with far too much time on their hands have discovered that, in the United Kingdom alone, around 40 per cent of women between 16 and 49 are celibate at any given time.

YOU MEAN I CAN WATCH THE FOOTY AS WELL?

How To Drive A Man Insane With Desire

- Meet him at the door in nothing save skimpy underwear and high heels. It'll shock the hell out of him, especially if you've just arrived from the office.
- Shout "No" in his ear when you really mean yes.
- Leave a trail of clothes from the living room to the bedroom and don't nag him to pick them up.
- Tell him you think he's God (and then refuse to have sex on account that it would be blasphemous).

- Hand him a picture of a nude centrefold during the middle of sex to save him having to fantasize about her.
- Pour warm beer all over your body and allow him to lick it off.
- Admire his manhood, preferably without squinting.
- Tell him you're going to bring your best friend to join in the fun, but don't tell him it's a hairdresser called Nigel.

Gutter Talk

To get more than just a penny for your thoughts, why not become a phone sex operator?

WHERE DID I PUT THOSE KEYS?

Sex Aids You Can Find In Your Handbag Without Getting Arrested

Spearmint Mouth Freshener Excellent source of nutrition for a busy working girl.

Piece of Fruit Useless for anything else but sex.

Mini Pack of Tissues Good for wiping off fruit stains.

Condoms Surefire way to ensure he doesn't make a mess in your hair.

Alka Seltzer Aids indigestion after swallowing things too quickly.

Purse Good for storing your credit cards and any money purloined from his wallet.

Handcuffs Only really socially acceptable if you happen to be an undercover policewoman.

Spare Pair of Stockings Useful for sticking in his mouth to stop him squealing too loudly.

Spare Set of Keys Not the ones for the handcuffs, unfortunately.

Lip Balm Useless for curing chapped lips and even more useless as a lubricant to ease his hands out of the handcuffs.

Silk Scarf Makes a great sling for his dislocated shoulder after you've attempted to wrench him and the handcuffs away from the bedpost.

Loose change Great in case of emergencies, like ringing the locksmith so you can reclaim your handcuffs.

Shopping Tip

Before giving in to a male's request for anal sex, test his theory that it won't hurt much by first experimenting upon him with a modestly sized shrink-wrapped vegetable.

WAS WHAT GOOD FOR ME?

How To Fake An Orgasm Really Badly

1. *Yawn loudly while he gets into bed.*

2. *Feign tiredness when he turns off the light.*

3. *Start loudly reciting cricket scores during foreplay to stop yourself from falling asleep.*

4. *Take out your nail file prior to penetration and start pushing down your cuticles.*

5. *Turn on the TV during pivotal moment; affect deep absorption in whatever show might be on.*

6. *During afterglow bit, when he asks if it was good for you too, say that you found the plot a trifle contrived and the main protagonist unsympathetic.*

7. *Refuse to hug, cuddle or touch him.*

8. *When you're sure he's sulking, roll over and start snoring in a pointed manner.*

Other Potent Put-Downs For The Sexually Empowered

"Hurry up, the commercial break's nearly over."

"Did you know there's a crack in your ceiling?"

"Say when."

"I've heard men with small penises try hard in bed. And you *do!*"

"What was your name again?"

Vital Statistic

Rocket scientists posing as researchers have discovered that many women prefer to sleep alone because of their partner's annoying habits. Biggest bugbears apparently include him hogging the bed or covers; tossing and turning; or watching the telly (probably while she's trying to have sex with his friend).

2.2 GET WITH IT, ROMEO!

"Ten men waiting for me at the door?
Send one of them home, I'm tired."
Mae West

So this is it. The moment you've all been waiting for: a guide to finding Mr Right. This compelling and in-depth portrayal of perfect matches shows how compatibility between a boy and a girl is all down to genetic make-up, family upbringing, social conditioning, economic circumstance, emotional well-being and spiritual connection.

Yeah right. Pull the other one. Even good girls know that a man's suitability depends only upon whether she fancies him or not. Mr Right might be the romantic novelist's saving grace or the smug mantra of lithium-laden housewives everywhere, but finding him in real life is only marginally less difficult than trying to open a tin of soup-for-one with your teeth. Indeed, if he's tall, dark, rich and handsome, he's probably taken. If he's short, bald, broke and ugly, he's all yours.

Love in so many acts

Boy meets girl. Girl pretends not to notice him. Boy chases girl. Girl tries hard not to get caught. Boy woos her with flowers. Girl starts to smile. Boy sends her a love letter. Girl starts to swoon. Boy calls to check she's received it. Girl picks up the phone on the first ring. Boy starts getting cold feet. Girl wonders why. Boy says he wants things to slow down a little. Girl starts going out with her friends more. Boy starts feeling insecure. Girl feels sorry for him and gives him a second chance. Boy orders in pizza to celebrate. Girl pretends to feel flattered. Boy starts farting in bed. Girl objects to it loudly. Boy tells her to stop nagging. Girl stops having sex. Boy starts going out with his mates more. Girl eventually leaves him. Boy bawls. Girl howls even harder. Boy thinks she'll be back soon but starts screwing around just in case she isn't. Girl sits at home moping and watching the phone. Boy thinks she's over him so continues to screw around to forget the fact that she's a cruel-hearted bitch. Girl gets told off by her friends for mourning over a no-good loser. Boy gets told off by his new girls for treating them like shit. Girl decides to get on with her life. Boy begins to get drunk and maudlin. Girl starts going out more again and bumps into boy. Girl pretends not to notice him. Boy chases after her. Girl tries hard not to get caught. Boy woos her with a candle-lit dinner. Girl wonders why. Boy gives her an engagement ring. Girl starts to cry.

Romantic Gesture

To keep the romance alive in your relationship, kick your partner out of bed in the morning and tell him he can't get back in until he's made you a cup of tea.

I'LL HAVE THE LOBSTER, THANKS

Making A Meal Out Of First Dates

First dates are always hard work. For one thing, there's the necessary phone call to make to your token married girlfriend to ensure she's beside herself with envy. Then there's the essential trip to the hairdresser's to get the casually – but immaculately – tousled hairdo. Next it's the mandatory sojourn at the manicurist's to get your scarlet talons filed down to a more demure, less dangerous length. Then there's the frantic dash to a department store to find yourself a drop-dead-gorgeous but not too try-hard frock. And finally, there's the race to the chemist for a packet of condoms. Frankly, by the end of the day, and before the big night even starts, it's a wonder a bad girl has the energy to raise a fork to her mouth, let alone anything else.

How To Ensure You Get A Second Free Meal From Your First Date

- Ask him lots of questions about himself.
- Pretend to be interested in his answers.
- Laugh at his jokes.
- Refuse to talk about yourself.
- Silently imply that you've never had an orgasm.
- Using sign language, tell him you're still a virgin.
- Don't order the lobster.

Things To Say To Ensure You Don't Get A Second Date

- Order the lobster
- Tell him about your collection of teddy bears.
- Tell him about your collection of porcelain dolls.
- Tell him about your collection of guns.
- Tell him about your abortions.
- Tell him about your divorce.
- Tell him about your stay in a psychiatric hospital.
- Tell him about your children.
- Tell him about your desire to have children.
- Tell him that all your previous boyfriends dumped you.
- Tell him that you dumped all your previous boyfriends.
- Tell him about your stalking ex.
- Tell him about your fabulous career.
- Tell him about your brilliant salary.
- Ask him when he's going to call you next.

Handy Hint

To increase your chances of a second date, don't have sex.
Strengthen your will-power by wearing unattractive underwear.

CAN I BRING MY LABRADOR?

Blind Dates And How To Avoid Them

Blind dates are probably more predictable than coming down with food poisoning after eating poisonous food. You get a call from a well-meaning girlfriend, usually one who's happily engaged in a terminal twosome. She reckons that this time she's found the perfect man for you. Having heard this before, and having had to suffer the consequences as a result, you beg off by saying you can arrange your own love life thanks very much, now bugger off and goodbye. She gives him your telephone number anyway.

He calls and you reluctantly relent but only because you've just finished peeling your nail polish off and so don't have anything more constructive to do that evening.

Cut to a couple of hours later when you enter the restaurant wearing dark glasses and hoping that the gorgeous fellow behind the bar is your sight-unseen suitor. Instinctively though, you know damned well that the festering eyesore in the corner that you wouldn't touch with a white stick, let alone a barge pole is more likely to be him. So here's what you do after you've gulped down your lobster and polished off his wine

1. *Excuse yourself from the table.*

2. *Head straight for the toilets.*

3. *Check around for exit routes.*

4. *Force small window above toilet cistern open with heel of shoe and/or fist.*

5. *Exit via window, legs first (you still want to avail yourself of any drug offers from any toilet-goers next in line).*

6. *Fall into skip full of restaurant left-overs (read: poisonous food).*

7. *After inadvertently swallowing a tiger prawn, come up for air, brush yourself down, then head straight to the hospital for a salmonella jab.*

First Aid Tip

If you do bring a pet Labrador along on a blind date, never leave it outside the restaurant tied to the tailgate of a stranger's parked car.

GIRL WITH GSOH NEED ONLY APPLY

Classified Ads And Other Desperate Dating Techniques

It goes without saying that bad girls don't need any help when it comes to beating men off with their handbags. However, if there is a bit of a shortage of blokes – because of, say, a war or something – then here's what to do to keep yourself amused until the more desirable members of the gene pool come home on leave*.

*Even a war hero with one leg, an eye-patch and a bad case of the jitters has got to be more appealing than any man who has to advertise for a girlfriend.

Personal Classifieds

- Describe yourself as "shortish, plumpish, grey-haired, brown-eyed, 80-year-old Scorpio woman".
- Refuse to reply to any of the subsequent responses on the grounds that they're bound to be from perverts.
- Only answer ads from men who simply require "intelligent girl with GSOH".

Striking Out In Singles Bars

- Dress so your cleavage and legs are hidden at all times.
- Refuse to let any man buy you a drink.
- Snarl menacingly at any man who approaches you for the next dance.

Getting Yourself Banned From Dating Agencies

- Refuse to go out with anyone too young, too old, too fat, too skinny, too tall, too short, too rich, too poor, or too ugly.
- Refuse to go out with anyone else who's desperate.
- Refuse to put down a deposit until after you've met at least one decent candidate.

Putting Men Off On The Net

- Pretend you're a man.
- Pretend you're a transvestite.
- Pretend you're a cyber cop.

Wry Observation

Isn't it strange how friends who recommend you take out a personal classified or join a dating agency have never done it themselves?

ROSES ARE RED, VIOLETS ARE CHEAP

Breaking Hearts On Valentine's Day

Whoever first said that money can't buy love was obviously some underachieving, witless male who, hopefully, ended up having to spend a fortune on dating agency fees because all his girlfriends left him after his paltry performances on Valentine's Day.

Every bad girl knows what every man doesn't: the money he spends is directly proportionate to the amount of times you'll sleep with/talk to him.

So, to save you and your sweethearts from massive disappointment for yet another year, best take a pragmatic, calculated approach and follow this two-step program to instant financial and romantic gratification:

1. *Dump current lovers at least two days before the big event.*

2. *Moan to girlfriends and family members alike that you're going to kill yourself if you don't receive at least one valentine this year.*

This should see you swamped with thousands of unsolicited, priceless presents from all kinds of suitors, desirable or otherwise.

The Secret Admirer You can count on this undercover Romeo to send you the most lavish bouquet and the sappiest card. He's usually not so anonymous either. More often than not, he's the dweeb who's been mooching round your office desk for the past 12 months, or the creepy-looking commuter who stares longingly at you on the train every morning. Feed his obsession. Then take his pathetic profferings. Then ignore him again until February next year.

The Prodigal Ex It goes without saying that at least one old flame will burn a path to your door come Valentine's Day. Indeed, he'll use the event as a pathetic excuse to state the bleeding obvious and declare he was a complete and utter idiot for having left you. Capitalize on his former misdemeanours and accept his extravagant tokens of contrition with as much grace and compassion as you can muster. Then kick him out and tell him not to darken your doorstep again until your next bout of present-profiteering (say, Easter or Christmas or Birthday).

The Spurned Lover This one's always a sucker for a sentimental occasion that can remind him of love long lost. He'll definitely try to bribe you back with priceless presents, providing he's still in the denial phase and not the anger one. (NB Dead rats don't count. Neither do wreaths.) Milk his grief for all it's worth. Politely accept the ring, the car, and the deeds to the holiday house in Tuscany. Then gently tell him you're sorry but you cannot be bought.

The Hapless Boyfriend Don't expect your man of the moment to overwhelm you with mawkish messages and extravagant gifts. Because, as he'll so cleverly quote: "you should know I love you", or "I show my feeling 365 days of the year" or "big deal, I forgot". Think of his short-sighted complacency as a long-term investment by making this Valentine's Day so hideously traumatizing for him that come next February 14 he won't dare treat the day so glibly or as cheaply.

The Well-Meaning Girlfriend Profit from the nosy, interfering do-gooder female friend who, being stupid enough to believe you when you say you don't have any male admirers, takes it upon herself to send you a large, anonymous bunch of flowers just to build your hopes up in order that they can come crashing down again when you finally realize it's from someone you don't want to sleep with. To cheer yourself up, you can always brandish said bouquet about in an ostentatious manner so as to taunt and tease any male admirers you do actually have, thereby encouraging them to race out and buy you an even bigger one.

The Car Park Attendant On Valentine's Day, hard-nosed companies and ruthless corporations suddenly discover their sensitive female side and go all out to woo the world's womenfolk. Prepare to be deluged with horrible artificial roses and Black Magic chocolates from "generous" bosses. Though these trinkets have little resale value, you could always try to use them to instigate a lucrative sexual harassment suit.

What price love?

The only truly desirable Valentine's Day gifts are job promotions (if he's your boss), marriage proposals (if he's your boyfriend) and blank cheques (if he's stupid). However, should you be forced to set your sights on lesser tributes, then be sure to take great pains to point out to potential swains that:

- Flowers are only acceptable if they're delivered to you in a public place. (It's pointless to be presented them in the solitary confines of your home since only you, him and the kitchen sink will ever get to appreciate them.)

- Twelve long-stemmed red roses are hackneyed and clichéd – but then again, so are crimes of passion when you receive carnations instead.

- Anything pretending to be a flower housed in a clear plastic tube will be duly employed to beat the sender about the head. Ditto cuddly toys and balloons on sticks.

- Chocolates, no matter how solidly Belgian or how lovingly hand-made, will only be well-received if there's a very expensive engagement ring imaginatively hidden in one of them.

- Lingerie is good, though only if *you* get to pick it and providing *he* doesn't expect to be the only one to see you in it.

- While *parfum* is fine, *eau de toilette* is very likely to end up inside one.

- Jewellery is encouraged but does not include identity bracelets, pearl anythings or pendants featuring locks of his hair.

- Dinner is satisfactory (providing he's intelligent enough to have made a reservation at least 10 weeks before in order to actually get a table).

- A night at a five-star hotel is laudable so long as he doesn't automatically assume he's coming with you.

Thoughts don't count

Valentine's Day messages, in whatever form, are of sentimental value only. And, unfortunately, since the entire male population has yet to discover its emotions, let alone put them down on paper, prepare yourself for the worst.

- Newspaper classifieds addressed to "Snookums", "Baby Cakes" or "Pumpkin Head" should be dealt with brutally and swiftly – unless, of course, your name is Sharon and you are under the age of 16.

- Low-flying planes toting love-struck banners, city billboards citing terms of endearment or contestants declaring undying passion on daytime game shows should be studiously ignored since any man who goes to such lengths is clearly desperate.

- "Luv" means never having to say you're sorry when you leave him because **a)** he obviously can't spell and **b)** he's got a problem with commitment.

- "Love always" means he's about to leave you. Or already has.

- Self-penned poetry is revolting unless its writer is a professional – which, in turn, means you won't be wanting his attention anyway as everybody knows that poets are a bunch of sad losers.

- Anything starting with the words "roses are red..." should be binned immediately.

Droll Comment
To become instantly more attractive to the opposite sex, why not get married?

WHILE YOU'RE DOWN THERE...CAN YOU SCRUB THE FLOOR?

Accepting Marriage Proposals With Extreme Bad Grace

Man does not deign to bend over and clean the toilet. Man would not dream of stooping to scour the bathtub. And man definitely never gets down on all fours to scrub the kitchen floor. So, any man who suddenly drops to bended knee and in quivering tones asks you to become his wife deserves to be treated with a five-minute fit of hysterical, unashamedly cynical laughter – particularly if he's doing it in public. Of course, should you start to feel a little unkind, you can always back-pedal a bit with follow-up words like "you", "have", "got", "to", "be" and "joking" followed by "I'm", "not", "going", "to", "be", "your", "bloody", and "housemaid".

When to refuse his hand in marriage:

- He lives at home with his parents.
- He lives in a pigsty by himself.
- His mum does his washing.
- His mum doesn't do his washing.
- He works away a lot.
- He works from home a lot.
- He's just lost his job.
- He doesn't have any money.
- He has money but won't let you spend it.
- He doesn't have a pension.
- He doesn't have any life insurance.
- He's already married.
- He's been married before.

- He's got kids.
- His kids don't like you.
- His ex-wife doesn't like you.
- His current wife doesn't like you.
- His physical disabilities are immense.
- His physical disabilities are hereditary.
- He drinks too much.
- He's a teetotaller.
- His breath smells.
- He snores in bed.
- He's crap in bed.
- His favourite hobby is watching the TV.
- His second favourite love is watching the football on TV.
- The ring doesn't come with a 30-day, no-questions-asked, money-back guarantee.

When to accept his hand in marriage:

- He begs, pleads, cajoles, sobs, cries and threatens to kill himself, and then only if you really, really fancy him.
- He writes you out a very large "cash only" cheque beforehand.
- You haven't got anything better to do for the rest of your life.

Golden Rule
Always test engagement rings for authenticity. If you can chew through it, it's good gold. If you lose a tooth, it's a decent diamond.

2.3 WHY WHITE WILL NEVER BE THE NEW BLACK

"My grandmother was a very tough woman.
She buried three husbands and two of them were just napping."
Rita Rudner

Black rules. White sucks. The only thing white you'll ever see on a bad girl is her face when she finds out her fiancé is digging his heels in and refusing to elope, or her husband is standing his ground and refusing to have a vasectomy.

Deep down, even without ever having walked down the aisle or had her legs up in stirrups, bad girls know that white doesn't equal good virtue, innocence and peace. White equals misery, pain, and hideously expensive dry-cleaning bills. White means wedding dresses laced with claret and christening gowns doused in colic. Moreover, white spells a man with romantic ideals far greater than his ability to carry them out all by himself.

Even if your intended has the soul of a poet, he'll have managed to turn you into a nagging fishwife and a scolding shrew long before you've reached the altar or left the maternity ward.

While he disappears for extended periods of time to search for pots of gold at rainbow's end or seek out the elves at the bottom of the garden, you can set about booking registry offices, hiring gynaecologists, firing photographers, dealing with interfering family members and midwives, and generally banging on about how christenings and weddings suck. Particularly white ones. Particularly your own.

Environmental Hazard

Never, ever consider marrying a conservationist or else you will be the only bride in Western civilization expected to get to your own wedding on a bicycle.

GETTING TO THE CHURCH ON LITHIUM

How The Best-Laid Wedding Plans Can Be Ruined By Reality

Trying to avoid pre-wedding jitters when you have a man by your side is like trying to avoid a Mormon in Utah. Possessed with the attention span of a five-year-old, the memory capacity of an old-age pensioner and the romantic nous of a brick, he wouldn't be able to organize a love-in in an ashram, let alone the 250-person extravaganza you originally had in mind. A man will get under your feet while you're being fitted for your dress, he'll turn up an hour late to the last-minute church rehearsals – and he'll vanish altogether when you demand to know which idiot took it upon himself to hire a donkey and cart instead of the horse-drawn carriage you'd initially envisaged.

It's only a piece of paper

If you're taking the plunge you might find yourself fretting over more profound matters than who sits where at the reception. Indeed, you may be shedding great buckets of tears, locked as you are in a deadly, destructive power-struggle over the writing of the wedding vows. It's not that you don't appreciate his promise to love, honour and obey you, it's just that the clause he wants to add at the end – the one that says "except when I feel like shagging my secretary" – seems a bit of a tall order. Especially when he refuses to let you have a get-out clause of your own – the one that says "in which case, I'm perfectly within my rights to string you up by your testicles."

Likewise, if you've hitched yourself to the tailcoats of a well-heeled, well-connected bloke you'll be far too busy squabbling over the pre-nuptial agreement he's had drawn up to worry about why you agreed to marry him in the first place. He think it's more than fair that you laugh loudly and heartily at his appalling jokes when he makes his wedding speech in return for the massive amounts he's willing to spend on what is shaping up to be the society event of the decade. Reluctant to sell your soul for monetary gain, you'll acquiesce on the proviso that he lets you have three more flower girls in the bridal party.

You're not going out in that!

From any bad girl's point of view, the only good thing about getting married is that you've got a great excuse to buy a new frock. The only bad thing about it is that unless white taffeta ballgowns make an unexpected, unwelcome comeback on the streets, you'll probably never want to wear it again. Furthermore, it's virtually impossible to exchange it the next day for a full refund without spending your entire wedding night trying to get claret stains out of the skirt. Smart-thinking, forward-looking brides-to-be tend to shun traditional gowns and opt for contemporary designs and colours instead.

- A short, black, cocktail dress is extremely versatile and its shade is more likely to reflect the mood leading up to your wedding day.
- A grey, mid-length, A-line pinafore can appear dreary but it hides unflattering bulges and you can wear it to school next term.

- A long, red, leather dress has limited wear though it's guaranteed to get you a double-page spread in the local newspaper.
- A bikini of any shape, size or colour will always come in handy, particularly when you're down at the beach.

Once you've bought your wedding gown, had all the numerous and pointless re-fittings and are now howling like a newborn babe because the idiot woman at the bridal shop never took into account the quantity of alcohol you'd consume during the nights leading up to the big day, it's time to frantically scour around for:

Something old – *can include the bridegroom if he's over 40, or his suit if he's had to hire it.*

Something new – *can include the wedding dress if you haven't been emotionally blackmailed into wearing a hand-me-down.*

Something borrowed – *can include the bridegroom if his divorce still hasn't come through yet, or, if you're a chronic chain-smoker, one of the bridesmaid's lighters (so long as you promise to return it).*

Something blue – *can include the torrent of swear words that come out of your mouth when you put on your wedding dress and discover you can neither sit, walk, talk, smile, drink, eat or breathe in it.*

A word of warning: if you've hooked up with a real man's man, expect him to demand a say in how you look on your wedding day. As he so charmingly puts it, "all girls should be seen and not heard." Consequently, he'll lumber you with the bridal equivalent of a body bag "so the priest can't look at your legs."

Worse still, the same neanderthal will scrutinize the gift list and add such essential matrimonial items as mop, bucket, apron and breast pump. Fortunately, he will let you choose the DJ ("but none of that poofter music, mind") because he'll have turned his tiny brain to the organization of the most important event in the forthcoming nuptials: hiring 12 kegs, five strippers and two cans of shaving cream. After all, that's certainly no job for a lady.

Nobody eats the food at weddings

A new-age, sensitive type will concentrate himself on less macho chores – like the catering. Of course, there's only so much he can do from the labyrinthine depths of the couch in front of the TV but, while you're running yourself ragged around town, he's sure to be holding a menu and ruminating over whether to choose the chicken or the seafood, or both. This would be useful, perhaps, if it were the wedding menu he was deliberating over, but it's not. It's a pizza delivery pamphlet he found under a cushion. (Important note: if he does ever manage to haul himself off the couch and start to move toward the door with purpose and intent, it's only because he's planning to gatecrash your kitchen tea.)

There is the occasional man who will be a bit better at organizing any event involving wine, women and a bowl of peanuts – especially if he's been married several times already. However, he's probably also trying to angle for an invite to the hen's night ("because all your friends have great tits") and allotted three-quarters of the entire catering budget to alcohol ("because it's a well-known fact that nobody eats the food at weddings"). In no time at all you'll realize why all his other wives eventually ran off with the best man.

Having said all this, beware of the bloke who stands by his word and really does look after every last little detail for you. At first, his offers to write out the wedding invitations entirely by hand and ensure that each muslin bag contains an equal amount of sugar-coated almonds will seem helpful – thoughtful even. That is, until you realize that it's only because he's a skinflint who doesn't want to incur any unnecessary costs. Warm and fuzzy feelings will wear completely thin when he then itemizes every single, sodding expense (including the wedding gown he pressured you into buying from a thrift shop) and starts whining about your profligate spending.

A quick word about the women

As soon as you've said yes to your grateful lover, your mother will race out and hire the photographer, the stylist, the lighting technician, the hairdresser, the make-up artist and the *haute couture* designer. She will, of course, remember to organize the same services for you. When you gently point out to her that it's you – and *only* you – who should be the main attraction on the big day, she'll go into an enormous sulk and accuse you of stealing her moment of glory.

And speaking of unwelcome intrusions, there's also That Woman who pokes her nose into the flower arrangements, storms off in a huff over your choice of bridesmaids, and hangs upon you because you refuse to wear her family heirloom (read: lace monstrosity) up the aisle. She's the mother of the man who is sure to get cold feet if you can't get on with her. And because she instinctively knows this, she'll feel duty-bound to tut-tut her disapproval at every suggestion you make. Best to leave all the bridal arrangements to her – and just hope that your own wedding invitation gets lost in the mail.

Things to do on your wedding day:

- Take a Valium to calm your nerves and then pass out at the altar.
- Arrive at the church three hours late in the hope that everyone has gone home.
- Put the organist through his paces by running down the aisle.
- Slur or mumble your words during the marital vows.
- Start snorting and guffawing most unattractively when the celebrant rattles off all the things you should solemnly declare.
- Throw the bouquet straight up in the air so you can catch it yourself.
- Ban any bridesmaid who is taller, prettier or slimmer from being in the official wedding snaps.
- Deliberately blink whenever the camera's about to flash.
- Defy male conventions and wedding traditions alike by making a speech at the reception.
- Heckle the bridegroom while he's making his.
- Look at the unmarried maid-of-honour's scandalous behaviour at the reception with more longing than is necessary.
- Kiss the best man with more gusto than is necessary.
- Slap the bridegroom when he kisses the maid-of-honour for longer than is polite.
- Do the bridal waltz in two-step.
- Insist that guests eat every last mouthful of the wedding cake before leaving so that you're not stuck with it.

Get Out Clause

If your wedding does turn out to be a dreadful disappointment you can always just pretend it was a particularly lavish date and get an annulment afterwards.

STOP THE PLANE, I WANT TO GET OFF

What To Expect On Your Honeymoon

After a tumultuous courtship and a roller-coaster wedding, you'll probably feel you deserve to sit back, relax and enjoy some happier moments with your fellow on a deserted island beach somewhere. Dream on. It's only when you whip off your wedding dress and whip out your rose-tinted sunglasses, that the trouble between you both really starts to take off. And that's because your man will only ever decide to reveal his most unlovable character traits the minute you touch down in paradise – or Preston, as the case may be.

The Chauvinist Pig

Don't expect to be wined and dined and then ravished at length by this old-fashioned sort. For starters, you'll be the one cooking the lobster, mixing the cocktails, fetching his slippers, sorting his socks and wondering why, when you mention the word "foreplay" he just looks at you and says "Huh?" Let's face it. Romance isn't really in this lug's lexicon – though, come to think of it, neither is any work of more than three letters and one syllable. In fact, it would be fair to say that the conjugal act could be over quicker than you can say "and I got married for *that*?" (You won't offend him by asking him this question, since he probably won't be able to understand sentences longer than his you-know-what.)

The Eternal Child

With this man, you'd best take precautions and reduce a long and lingering three-week honeymoon to an extremely short and snappy dirty weekend. Even then, he'll probably get bored very quickly. So, to revive his flagging interest and your fledgling marriage, tempt him with plenty of love-making variety in lots of exotic locations: kiss him inside a tunnel, have foreplay on top of a precipice, climax in a speeding train and bathe in the afterglow under a shower of water. Quite frankly though, if the honeymoon is not on Magic Mountain in Disneyland, I really don't fancy your chances.

The Mummy's Boy

Dear Mummy: This evening I am stuck on a remote desert island with my new bride. Weather is hot, the sharks are friendly and my wife is lovely (but not as lovely as you, of course). I am sorry I had to refuse your kind offers of chaperoning me here on my honeymoon. Unfortunately, my wife (rather meanly, I thought) said she didn't want "that interfering old battle-axe banging on the wall of the hut next door to check her precious son is still breathing." Anyway, I'd better sign off now because my wife is casting me black looks. She reckons three postcards to you in one day is more than enough. Wish you were here. Your favourite son.

The Perpetual Teenager

Honeymooner's disease (or any other one you're likely to catch off him) is the least of your problems when it comes to the man equipped with roving eye, bucket mouth and bad taste in music. Since he tends to act less than his age, you may need to spell out a few dos and don'ts while you're in Las Vegas*: "Don't touch any female except for me." "Do keep your trap shut and your wallet closed." Otherwise by the end of your stay, he'll have got half the strippers pregnant, argued and then fought with most of the Mafia and lost your mortgage deposit on the blackjack table.

*Where else would a man who doesn't take wedding vows very seriously and likes watching Elvis Presley impersonators take you?

The Rebel

While you might be used to him flaunting the rules of convention in order to make the world a better place (while simultaneously ensuring your life is made as awful as possible), when it comes to planning your honeymoon, don't back down on your less high-minded notions of what constitutes newly-wedded bliss. No matter how much he begs, cajoles and wheedles, there is nothing romantic or noble about catching dysentery or diptheria in under-rated beauty spots [insert appropriate Third World country here] or being bitten by an endangered species in untouched wilderness [insert appropriate snake-infested South American jungle here].

The Narcissist

WARNING: before you leave for your honeymoon with this man, for goodness sake hide your camera. And don't let him try to buy one in duty-free. While other men use their Pentax for faking holiday snapshots of famous landmarks or of you in your sexy new lingerie (brought specifically for the occasion), this man will insist you take pictures of him in his leopard skin G-string, and nowhere near the Statue of Liberty because she's not as impressive to look at. Never mind that you're scowling behind the lens and wondering when he's going to stop showing off and get down to conjugal duties – to his way of thinking, you're damned lucky to be the one pressing the button.

The Workaholic

If you want romance on your honeymoon, and you haven't been able to catch the handsome bellboy's eye or inspired the passion of a passing waiter, here's hoping you've packed a week's supply of Mills and Boon as well as a rechargeable, donkey-sized vibrator. Because if hubby's a workaholic, he'll be too busy taking high-powered business calls on his mobile to be be able to whisper sweet nothings into your ear. This would be acceptable perhaps if he had the good manners to put callers on "Hold" at the climactic moment. After all, the last thing you want is his high-powered clients and colleagues hearing how much fun a girl can have with an equally as high-powered battery.

The Nag

Don't expect the earth to move too much if your bridegroom is the sort who prefers sweeping the floor rather than sweeping you off your feet. Indeed, while you're lying seductively – albeit murderously – on top of the jumbo-size bed, he'll be firing off detailed reports to hotel management complaining about the disgraceful amount of dust he's just found under it. If on the off-chance he does manage to put down his pen and rise to the occasion so to speak, let's just say that it's probably the perfect time to start compiling your duty-free shopping list. Oh, and if he does let you clamber on top for a change, don't be too grateful. He's probably only doing it in order to check the ceiling for cobwebs.

The Closet Homosexual

This one will be too busy stocking up on his already cram-packed trousseau to bother about hot and heavy petting sessions with his delightful new bride, despite loudly muttered sexual slurs from your good self about not realizing you had landed yourself with a gay bloke.

But, after he's finally finished fingering the lapels of his new Donna and Gianni and Yves and Georgio suits (and you've finished cutting the holes out of the pants), he might finally relent and run his hands up and down your own velvety skin.

The Lazy Lump of Lard

Some men have voracious appetites. Unfortunately, none of them are likely to have anything to do with making mad, passionate, energetic love on a wind-swept beach – unless, of course, you're smart enough to entangle yourself in nutrition-rich seaweed or you've bought the bottle of chocolate-flavoured body-paint along. Only then will he leave the hotel room, lumber down to the seashore and make a heavy-handed lunge. It would be fair to say that this man won't get out of the marital bed for less than 10,000 calories a day.

The Useless Waste of Space

Of course, some men couldn't organize a quick shag in a Newcastle motor inn, let alone a long, languorous, lust-filled honeymoon in Fiji – which is why he'll probably have to settle for a stony silence when you arrive at your holiday destination, start desperately scanning the place for swaying palm trees and coconut daiquiris but find nothing save a down-at-heel concrete guesthouse in some godforsaken suburb. Of course, if your bridegroom is a true romantic at heart, he's sure to make the best of a bad situation by pointing out the inner beauty of a roach-riddled mattress and the sentimental value of the fair-sized rat that appears from behind the broken-down bar fridge. Look on the bright side yourself: you can always file for divorce when you get back home.

NOT ANOTHER SODDING TOASTER

Marriage Guidance For Beginners

The honeymoon is over and you've just finished unwrapping the wedding gifts. The vast and dismaying assortment of small electrical kitchen appliances laid out before you should tell you that married life is going to be about as exciting as a three-point plug. However, don't attach the brand-new electric bread knife to your wrists just yet.

Like your mother's always told you, there's a lot to be said for a safe, solid, stable, secure relationship. Of course, it's easy for her to say that, now she's happily divorced. But unlike her, at least from now on you'll always have someone to go to the supermarket with (and nag you for refusing to buy home brand items) and you'll never have to worry what to do on Saturday nights (take-away curry, action or horror movie on video, and lights out by 11).

Seven steps to less trouble and strife

1. *Answer all his strident rhetoric about world affairs over the breakfast table with a 'Yes, dear' and carry on reading your paper.*

2. *Padlock the fridge, the garage and the television remote control.*

3. *Take charge of all money-handling tasks. This includes the collecting and keeping of all wages and the paying of all credit card and store card bills.*

4. *Avoid telling him the real price you paid for any item of clothing, jewellery or ready-prepared supermarket meal.*

5. Act like a maid in the bedroom, a cook in the lounge and a slut in the kitchen, so he never gets complacent.

6. Never ask him if he had a good day at the office unless you want to be bored witless for the rest of the evening.

7. Don't invite single, divorced or recently widowed women to your dinner parties unless you want to start feeling resentful and bitter about your own less exciting status.

Marital Advice

Return any wedding gift which comes with a plug attached or with batteries included (vibrators excepted, of course).

Gratuitous Bloke Joke

What do women do with their arseholes? Give them a packed lunch and send them to work.

NINE MONTHS OF HARD LABOUR

Milking Your Pregnancy For All It's Worth

A bad mum-to-be falls into one of two distinct categories:

1. *The one who wants babies because they look extraordinarily cute decked out in miniature designer togs.*

2. *The one who doesn't want babies because she'll never be able to afford nice clothes for herself again.*

Obviously if you fall into the first category, you'll see pregnancy purely as an inconvenient means to a more hopeful end. But, if you're cynical from the outset, then you're in trouble.

Girls who fall into the second category don't view the ominous hues on the home pregnancy indicator as a welcoming excuse to start shopping for baby clothes. Indeed, if news of the baby's imminent and high-maintenance arrival isn't bad enough, you're then expected to quit smoking, stop drinking, get fat, throw up and attend ante-natal classes just for the privilege of deciding to keep the little critter.

The G Spot
Giving up on men and taking a female lover instead can often seem appealing and less trouble – until you figure out that she'll probably be as demanding as you in bed.

A day in the life of a bad mum-to-be

10am Lie in bed in a bad mood as you have just tried to quit smoking again.

10.15am Throw up.

10.30am Throw up again, but decide to blame it on the six Sea Breezes drunk the night before.

11am Still in bed in a bad mood as you have decided never to drink again.

11.15am Throw up.

11.30am Throw up.

11.45am Try to get up but sight of maternity clothes inspire fit of lethargy caused by pre-natal depression.

12noon Throw up.

12.15pm Get up, eat dry toast and sip a cup of black tea in the hope of quelling nausea.

12.30pm Throw up.

1.00pm Decide nausea is not the result of excessive alcohol consumption after all, so have fortifying glass of champagne.

1.15pm Throw up.

1.30pm Try Lucozade instead.

1.45pm Throw up.

2.00pm Attempt to scrub toilet but can't bend down because of extended stomach.

2.15pm Throw up.

2.30pm Attempt to scrub toilet again.

2.45pm Sneak cigarette.

3.00pm Throw up.

3.15pm Decide to do some housework.

3.16pm Forget to do the housework thanks to helpful, pregnancy-induced forgetfulness

3.30pm Throw up.

3.45pm Decide to go to bed to avoid throwing up again.

5.45pm Wake up feeling much, much better. Light up another illicit cigarette.

5.46pm Throw up.

6.00pm Partner comes home to find weeping great bundle on the floor in the kitchen.

6.15pm Throw up as partner starts cooking dinner.

6.30pm Head for ante-natal classes to practise inhaling gas.

7.00pm Thrown out for lighting up cigarette during tea break.

7.15pm Throw up.

7.30pm Return home, get on scales and panic on account of high weight gain despite having not kept any food down for well over five months.

7.45pm Make yourself throw up.

8.00pm Go to bed and sleep.

10.00pm Practise for pending night feeds by making partner get up out of bed to fetch snacks from all-night supermarket.

10.15pm Eat three pickled beetroots, two large lumps of coal and a genetically-modified chocolate bar, then promptly throw up yet again.

10.30pm Fall asleep and dream about not throwing up any more.

Pregnant Pause

Childbirth is an ideal time to voice all your grievances to your partner without him taking it too personally.

THIRTY-SIX HOURS CAN SEEM LIKE A LIFETIME

A Crash Course In Childbirth

Expletives excluded and sound effects added, the secret to an easier labour can be summed up in five words: "I"... pant, pant, pant, puff, puff, puff... "WANT"... pant, pant, pant, scream... "A"...gasp, gasp, pant..."CAESAREAN"... puff, puff, squeal, scream..."NOW!!!"

Vital Statistic
Brain surgeons at Bristol University surveyed more than 7,000 parents and discovered that more women than men suffered from depression after the birth of their babies.

DRAGGING UP BABY

Basic Skills For Unsuitable Mothers

No bad-mum-to-be can do without this brief but essential guide to bawling brats. From suggestions for names to arguments for better birth control methods, babies are put on the chair and dissected at length, hopefully while they're still just a twinkle in daddy's eye.

Names to give to your child just for the hell of it

- Names that are hard to live down, like Heavenly Hiraani, Tiger Lily, Peaches or Fifi-Trixibelle.
- Names that are hard to live up to, including Elle, Claudia, Naomi or Brad.
- Names that sound like you're on drugs, such as Dweezil, River, Leaf or Twig.
- Names of American soap star characters such as Brick, Brook, Patch or Ridge.
- Names of Australian soap star characters like Darren, Narelle, Charlene or Kylie.
- Names of people that you don't like, such as Celine, Mariah or Whitney.
- Names that can only be spelt or pronounced by the Irish, the Welsh or Hollywood agents, like Sorcha, Ryhhhdyfffrdywfynth or De*mi*.
- Names that can never be spelt or pronounced, such as The Twit Formerly Known As Pop Star.
- Names to discourage them from playing football, like Cyril, Cedric, Rupert or Jane.

Excuses to make to friends when your child behaves badly

"He's got wind."

"He's got colic."

"He's overtired."

"He's just woken up."

"He's teething."

"He's hungry."

"He's thirsty."

"His nappy needs changing."

"He's scared of you."

"He's scared of me."

"He doesn't like being locked in the cellar."

"He's hyperactive."

"He's eaten too many of those sweets that you gave him."

"He's not usually like this."

"He's just found out he's adopted."

"He's extroverted."

"He's just being playful."

"He's over-excited."

"He's shy."

"He's feeling left out."

"He's a gifted child."

"He takes after me."

"He's trying to impress you."

"He's trying to impress me."

"He's drunk."

"He's just a kid."

"He's only a boy."

"He's a typical man."

"He's just like his father."

Ways to ensure your children end up in regression therapy when they're adults

- Bottle-feed rather than breastfeed.
- Make them change their nappies themselves.
- Teach them to swim by dropping them in the bathtub.
- Refuse to let them have the toy out of the breakfast cereal packet.
- Threaten to kill them.
- Smack them in public.
- Tell them they're adopted.
- Nick their sweets.
- Make them eat broccoli.
- Disguise the broccoli in a quiche.
- Leave IOUs in their piggy banks.
- Give them socks, underwear and large bags of tangerines for Christmas.
- Give them books for their birthday.
- Refuse to buy them a pony.
- Send them to school when they're not feeling very well.
- Send them to school wearing hand-me-downs.
- Tell the teacher when they're being bullied by other kids.
- Take them out of school because you've had a row with their teacher.
- Make them start a new school in the middle of term.
- Refuse to write them sick notes to get out of doing gym.
- Tell them off for losing their gym gear.
- Drag them out to see relatives on weekends.
- Make them stay in until they've finished their homework.
- Refuse to park a mile away from the school when you're picking them up.
- Refuse to let them leave school.
- Make them take a weekend job at a supermarket.

- Ban them from smoking.
- Tell them off for nagging you about your smoking.
- Make them introduce you to all their friends.
- Refuse to let them drink alcohol with their friends.
- Get drunk in front of their friends.
- Embarrass them in front of their dates.
- Don't let them out on a date.
- Encourage them to marry their date.

A Pre-cautionary Tale

To avoid depression, bloating, swelling, fatigue, weight gain, backache, stretch marks, haemorrhoids or varicose veins, always use a condom.

I WON'T MAKE THAT BLOODY MISTAKE AGAIN

Birth Control Methods For Mums With Bad Feelings

1. *Watch another woman giving birth.*

2. *Listen to another woman giving birth.*

3. *Remember the time you gave birth.*

4. *Only have sex on a leap year (or when the Olympics are on – which ever comes last).*

5. *Make your partner wear pyjamas to bed.*

6. *Wear flannelette nighties to bed.*

7. *Get a divorce.*

Decorating Tip
Why not turn unsightly objects in your house into objects of art by hanging your children on the wall?

2.4 IS THAT A GUN IN YOUR POCKET?

"The quickest way to a man's heart is through his chest."
Roseanne Barr

When lust turns to loathing, the battle of the sexes starts in deadly earnest. All the things about him that used to make your stomach flip now just make it turn.

Whereas one time you would rush to get into bed now you just rush to the bathroom. When once you would have trod broken glass to impress him, these days you spend most of your time clearing it up, all the while cursing yourself for wasting a perfectly good cut crystal vase on such a bleeding loser.

To ride out the bad times good girls are advised by those who know better to raise their heads high, button their lips and take a hold of their tongues. Bad girls don't have the same will-power, or respect for their mums.

When the enemy's standing in front of her, a bad girl is more likely to lower her head, open her mouth, take a hold of him and bite - really hard. That way at least she can be sure that "Till death do us part" takes on a more poignant and ear-shattering ring.

Reasons why relationships can go seriously wrong

1. *Sex* You don't want it with him.

2. *Affairs* He finds out about yours.

3. *Money* You spend too much of his.

4. *Work* He refuses to take any interest in yours.

5. *Family* You refuse to spend time with his.

6. *Children* He acts like one of them.

Candid Counsel

If and when you start having marital difficulties, always make sure your marriage guidance counsellor is a woman. That way you can both gang up on your husband.

TRUST ME, I'M A MAN

Sure Signs That He's Cheating On You

It's very difficult to get a bad girl to understand that when a man is fooling around she's supposed to be the *last* person to know, not the first. Unfortunately, all those years of being encouraged by women's intuition and magazines alike to snoop through wallets and pick locks on briefcases have made her a veritable lie-detector on legs – not to mention a pain-in-the-neck to live with on a day-to-day basis.

Every bad girl knows that the biggest three giveaways that he's having an affair are: lipstick on his collar (it's not your shade); blonde hairs on his jacket (they're fake, yours is natural); and B&B charges on his credit card (you only stay in hotels).

Other, more subtle, signs include:
- He's told you he is.
- He denies that he is.
- He accuses you of cheating on *him*.
- He arrives home reeking of perfume.
- He arrives home reeking of aftershave.
- He arrives home reeking of alcohol.
- He works late.
- He leaves for work early.
- He works at weekends.
- His mobile phone is always switched off.
- He dashes off to public phone boxes when there's a perfectly good phone in the house.
- Whenever he picks up the phone at home, it's a wrong number.
- Whenever you pick up the phone at home, the caller hangs up.
- He won't make love to you with the lights on.

- He won't make love to you even with the lights off.
- He suddenly wants to make love all the time.
- He buys you flowers.
- He buys himself a sports convertible.
- He's always vacuuming inside it.
- He starts being nice to you.
- He stops being nice to you.
- He starts going to the gym.
- He stops encouraging you to go to the gym.
- He starts encouraging you to spend time with your friends.
- He bursts into tears every time he hears a really crap love song.
- He bursts into tears every time he sees you.
- He suggests going to relationship counselling.
- He refuses to go to relationship counselling.
- He stops going to relationship counselling.
- He gets a new haircut.
- He doesn't notice your own.
- He starts wearing a toupée.
- He doesn't care when you fall about laughing over it.

Suspicious Comment

Never trust a man with a toupée, a beard, a moustache, a five o'clock shadow or a clean-shaven face.

I SPY SOMETHING BEGINNING WITH 'BASTARD'

Playing Amateur Detective With Professional Aplomb

1. *Turn out his pockets when washing clothes to check for unexplained love letters, photographs, and hair grips.*

2. *Check for magenta, apricot, cerise or fuschia-coloured marks on shirt collars and around broken trouser zips before taking suits to dry cleaners.*

3. *Intercept credit card statements and mobile phone bills.*

4. *If he's been on a business trip, intercept his hotel receipts and check for room service for two.*

5. *Check for sudden large drops in levels in his aftershave bottle.*

6. *Check car ashtray for lipstick-smudged cigarette butts.*

7. *Check backseat of car for stray hairs.*

8. *Befriend his company's receptionist (she can't lie so well on his behalf if she likes you).*

9. *Befriend his secretary on the off-chance she's the culprit (she'll act odd and jittery if she is).*

10. *Ring his office after hours to check if he's really working late.*

11. *Always ask how his day was and get him to relate it in detail.*

12. *Cross-reference his diary appointments with what he says he's been doing.*

13. *Check his diary for unusual entries (Julie, with five stars by the name, is often a dead giveaway).*

14. *Ring any phone numbers contained in his diary that do not have names next to them.*

15. *Listen in on all his phone calls at home on the extension.*

16. *Check his back nightly for strange scratches.*

17. *Check his neck and upper chest area for strange bites.*

18. *Check his left hand to see if he's still got his wedding ring on.*

19. *Leave obtrusive and unexpected things like skateboards and panes of glass lying around in your hallway during the dead of night so you know exactly what time he stumbles in.*

20. *Bluff him and tell him that someone saw him with some other woman. It's a long shot but he might just believe you and give the game away.*

Old Wives' Tale
The difference between good girls and bad girls is that good girls marry the men they sleep with.

WHERE'S MY PENTHOUSE THEN?

How to Fail Miserably At Being A Mistress

Unlike the good wife who has to rely upon a good friend to tell her that her husband's a deceitful swine, the bad girl instinctively knows that he can't be trusted – mainly because she's dating him behind the good wife's back. Of course, the betrayal is almost always short-lived, even without the help of the nasty piece of work masquerading as the good wife's good friend. Bad girls don't make very good mistresses. Bad girls like to cause a scene whereas bad husbands like to spend their entire lives trying to avoid one. In fact, it would be fair to say that the illicit affair lasts for about as long as the time it takes you to give him a love-bite that even the most blindly-loving spouse will spot.

Top 10 spots to find a married man of your very own

1. At the office.

2. In the gym.

3. At a singles bar.

4. In a conference hotel lobby.

5. At a church, waiting at the altar.

6. At the park walking the family dog.

7. *In a waiting room near the maternity ward.*

8. *Sitting inside a car outside a school at around 3.30pm.*

9. *Standing outside a marriage guidance office having a cigarette.*

10. *At your local YMCA.*

Lies he can tell you to make you cross

"My wife doesn't understand me."

"We're separated."

"She's asked me back."

"I've only done it for the sake of the mortgage."

"I've only done it for the sake of the kids."

"We don't have sex any more."

"I've never done this before."

"I feel so guilty about her."

"I feel so guilty about you."

"You deserve someone better than me."

"You deserve more than this."

"You deserve to be happily married with kids of your own."

"I wish I wasn't married – then I could be with you."

"I'll leave her as soon as Christmas is over."

"I'll leave her once my youngest has started school."

"I'll leave her once my youngest has finished school."

"I'll leave her once the grandkids have finished school."

"I'll leave her when I've got her settled into the retirement home."

"I can't leave her – it would kill her."

Ways to send him scuttling back to his wife

- Demand a penthouse or, at the very least, some rental assistance.
- Demand more housekeeping money than she does.
- Nag him.
- Refuse to sleep with him.
- Refuse to iron his business shirts.
- Refuse to check into hotels with him under his name.
- Request his home phone number – then ring it.
- Request he provide DNA evidence that he still doesn't sleep with his wife.
- Demand to celebrate Christmas, New Year's Eve, Valentine's Day or his wife's birthday with him.
- Ask him to spend an entire evening with you.
- Ask him to leave her.

Vital Statistic
Statistics suggest that women initiate four out of five divorces. The wife probably instigates the fifth one.

DARLING, I'M HAVING AN AFFAIR

Cuckolding Men in Three Easy Lessons

When it comes to the topic of infidelity, most men are so smug and self-satisfied about the monogamous leanings of the fairer sex, they wouldn't believe you were cheating even if you were fool enough to tell them. Short of actually taking the photographs yourself and slapping the negatives down on his breakfast tray, or wandering around the house with naught but a whopping great scarlet letter 'A' stamped on your forehead and an outraged lynch mob from *News of The World* following closely behind, it's virtually impossible to get found out.

However, if perchance you do happen to have married a man who is genuinely humble and can't understand why you're going out with him rather than someone rich, witty, charming and good-looking, then you're going to have to take a few precautionary measures:

1. **Get yourself an alibi.** *Preferably a female friend with ongoing "marital problems" and "suicidal tendencies". It'll help if she lives at least 50 miles away, has no other friends or family to rely upon and has just had her phone cut off because of extreme financial difficulties. That way you can easily account for long, frequent and often expensive absences and, at the same time, feed your husband's fantasy about you being a paragon of virtue.*

2. **Stop sleeping with your husband.** *It's very hard for women to divorce their feelings from the act of sex. Wincing, grimacing or rolling your eyes during lovemaking sessions with your partner is hardly going to allay his suspicions.*

3. **Always deny any wrongdoings.** *Don't ever crack under pressure and confess. Because they're so competitive, men rarely forgive straying partners for trying to outdo them in the adultery stakes. Even if your man has received a very reliable eye-witness report (his mother saw you canoodling outside a local hotel, when you were supposed to be on a suicide watch in Timbuktu), just bite your bottom lip, stare at him so hard that tears start to well in your eyes and whisper "I am immensely hurt that you believe that scheming, manipulative lying old bag over me." This should shame him into shutting up nicely.*

Lies you can tell any trusting man

"I didn't realize what time it was."

"I did call but the phone was engaged."

"Then I must have dialed the wrong number, mustn't I?"

"I stayed at a friend's house."

"Of course I love you."

"Oh, alright then."

"Yes, it was good for me too."

"No. There's nothing wrong."

"It's not you, it's me."

"No. There's no-one else involved."

"I just need a little time to think things over, that's all."

"Okay, I promise. I'll be back next week."

"I miss you too."

"I'll be back the week after."

"Oh, alright, if it means that much to you."

"God, the house is a pigsty."

"Of course I missed you."

"Yes, it's good to be back."

"Yes, I thought the counselling session was productive too."

"Won't be long. I'm just popping out for a packet of fags."

Cheat's Note

Always call the speaking clock immediately after calling a long-distance lover. That way, when your suspicious live-in lover hits the "Redial" button on the telephone, he'll just think you're an obsessive timekeeper rather than an adulterous cow.

CAN YOU CALL ME A CAB, PLEASE?

50 Ways to Leave Your Lover

The reason men behave badly is because most girls don't behave badly *enough*. Screaming obscenities and throwing knives doesn't count. Even the least patient of men will put up with that kind of scene in a restaurant so long as he's guaranteed a shag over the table afterwards.

No, the most effective way to keep him on his toes is to leave him. (NB: Don't worry if you don't succeed the first time. Practice will make perfect the second.)

1. *Resolutely pack your bags while your partner heeds icy request to call a cab.*
2. *Go outside to wait for the cab, ignoring silent pleas from distraught, though still not as yet visibly repentant, partner.*
3. *Go back inside house 20 minutes later and call cab company to find out where cab is.*
4. *Exit house again, accidentally stepping on tail of partner's dog for dramatic effect.*
5. *Walk slowly but resolutely toward taxi cab.*
6. *Feign surprise when partner comes racing after you.*
7. *Reluctantly give taxi cab driver a small cancellation fee.*
8. *Briefly acknowledge he's good-looking in an unkempt, uneducated sort of way but argue over the size of the tip anyway.*
9. *Have reconciliatory sex (with partner, not cab driver).*
10. *Apply antiseptic cream to carpet burn.*
11. *Listen to declarations of undying love while sipping electrolyte supplement for sudden and chronic attack of cystitis.*
12. *Unpack bags again.*
13. *Make up with dog.*

14. Kick dog off bed in the middle of the night.

15. Kick partner out of bed in the morning.

16. Enjoy full English breakfast he's whipped up using every dish in the house.

17. Argue over who's going to do the dishes.

18. Read evening paper while he's still doing dishes.

19. Kick dog off bed again.

20. Have more reconciliatory sex (with partner, not dog).

21. Eventually beg off with a headache.

22. Put up with quiet sulks from his side of the bed.

23. Have sex in the morning to keep him quiet.

24. Get up to avoid having to lie in the wet patch again.

25. Run bath.

26. Lay out clothes.

27. Make pot of coffee.

28. Wonder why he can't do all of this for himself.

29. Decide that nothing has really changed.

30. Feed dog.

31. Decide that something has to change.

32. Ask partner if he loves you.

33. Ask him when he's going to make an honest woman of you.

34. Ask him when he's going to give you a baby.

35. Receive patronising kiss on forehead in response to all three of the previous questions.

36. Throw cup of freshly brewed coffee at his retreating back.

37. Realize why you wanted to leave him in the first place.

38. Stare at dog malevolently for a while.

39. Fail to notice dog cringing.

40. Call in sick to work.

41. Call your mother.

42. Call your friends.

43. Listen to their advice about all men being the same.

44. Refuse to heed any of it.

45. Pack bags again.

46. Press "Redial" on the phone.

47. Promise taxicab company you really mean to leave this time.

48. Kick dog on the way out again to get the taxi.

49. Notice it's the same cab driver and he's still good-looking in an unkempt, uneducated sort of way.

50. Climb into taxicab and drive away.

Pet's Corner

Only buy short-legged dogs so they can't jump on to your bed.

DEAR JOHN, YOU'RE DROPPED

Writing Heart-Felt Break-Up Letters

Breaking some-one's heart is never easy. That's why men try to do it telepathically. Girls, at least, have a little more respect for their about-to-be-jilted lovers. Working under the, often misguided, belief that the pen is politer than cold silences, more convenient than disappearing acts and less hassle than yanking the phone from the wall, a woman writes her misgivings down on paper. She then proceeds to waste acres of pine plantations, all the while fretting about mixed messages and agonizing over split infinitives. So, to save you the grief and to help you get on with your new life without him, here's a cut-out-and-keep collection of personalized, copyright-free and photocopy-as-often-as-you-like letters for you to post, fax, e-mail or send via the bailiffs.

Dear John
Em, after receiving this, you'll probably wish your name were anything but.
Love

....
[sign here]

Dear John – oops, sorry – Richard
I'm leaving you for another.
Love

....
[sign here]
PS Bet you can't guess his name!!!

Dear John

Sorry this is by fax rather than by post, but I'm in a hurry to leave.

Love

....

[sign here]

Dear John

Sorry I couldn't deliver this in person but my solicitor suggested that sending a bailiff would be deemed more appropriate.

Love

....

[sign here]

PS Please see divorce papers attached.

Dear Jon

Sorry I had to e-mail thiss instead ov writing you a proper leter but my spellling sux!!! As do you.

Luv

....

[Insert name here]

Gratuitous Bloke Joke

How many men does it take to wallpaper a room? One, if you slice him thinly enough.

SIX NEAT GINS AND A THREE-PLY TISSUE

Coping With Grief Made Easy

Okay. After all the squabbles, quarrels, arguments, shouting, screaming, yelling, tantrums and emergency casualty-ward visits, he's gone and done the unthinkable. He's left you. And he says he's never coming back. While this might be the moment you've dreamt about every night for the past five years of your rocky relationship, it comes as a bit of a shock when it actually happens. Especially since, in *your* dreams, you were the one who dropped *him*.

To help you cope during the messy aftermath of a relationship break-up, here's a brief outline of the six stages of grieving and how each is likely to manifest itself.

Stage 1 - Disbelief

(as in "But I *love* you, you bastard.")

Refuse to believe that he means what he says.
- Tell your family and friends what a bastard he is anyway.
Drink six neat gins to make yourself feel worse.

Stage 2 - Denial

(as in "He's cracking, I can tell.")

Pretend you're still going out with him and call him every evening when you're drunk.

Pretend to your family and friends that you and he are trying to patch things up.

Pretend that you aren't developing a drink dependency.

115

Stage 3 - Guilt
(as in "Maybe I'll get him back if I grovel hard enough.")

- Pretend to feel bad about hanging up on him when he tried to reason with you during the denial stage.
- Pretend to feel remorseful about bad-mouthing him to your family and friends during the disbelief stage.
- Pretend to feel contrite about downing a further three bottles of gin during this stage.

Stage 4 - Anger
(as in "I can't believe I just grovelled to him for absolutely nothing.")

- Hurl abuse down the phone and on to his answering machine during the day.
- Bang on his door late at night when you're drunk and threaten to batter him to death with the rock you found in his garden if he doesn't take you back.
- Put the rock through the window when you realize he's out.

Stage 5 - Acceptance
(as in "He's ruining my life and I'm not even getting a shag out of it.")

- Realize that your phone and your drink bills are going through the roof.
- Realize that your family and friends are about to disown you.
- Realize that he is not coming back.

Stage 6 - Resolution
(as in "I'm going to get myself a new man. That'll fix him.")

- Decide to get a bridging loan for the phone bill and the booze.
- Decide to play hard to get by bypassing his place in future.
- Decide to get a new hair cut and go to the gym.

Diet Tip

If you need to lose a lot of weight quickly, have a tumultuous break-up with your boyfriend.

REVENGE IS A DISH BEST SERVED WITH BABY FOOD

Five Ways to Really Get Back At Him

Men. You can't live with them, and you can't force them into a bath of battery acid and then bury the remains under the patio in your back garden. At least not without the whole bloody world getting to know about it. So you've got to think of more discrete ways to make him suffer.

From leaving his phone off the hook after dialing the speaking clock in Brazil, to sprinkling his pre-moistened carpets with cress seeds and then turning the heating up, urban myths abound about ways bad girls quietly get their own back on callous cads.

However, if your man's smart enough to have put a bar on the phone and cork tiles on the floor, here's a few other satisfying, though not as widely-talked-about, acrimonious actions to add to your list of things-to-do-before-he's-dead:

1. *Get pregnant and refuse to have an abortion.*

2. *Get pregnant and make him pay for all your maternity clothes.*

3. *Get pregnant and flatly refuse to put his name down on the baby's birth certificate.*

4. *Get pregnant and then refuse him access to the baby.*

5. *Get pregnant and demand child-maintenance payments.*

Obviously, these tactics rely upon man being a very predictable beast who, after coldly ditching you, will still have no qualms about sleeping with you providing that you ask nicely enough or act pathetically enough.

Dirty Thought
If you do finally relent and let your male deserter see his new-born baby, take care to hand it over just after feeding time.

DIAL 'M' FOR MANSLAUGHTER

Fantasy of a Vengeful Wife

SOUND OF BAD GIRL DIALING A PHONE NUMBER.

OPERATOR: *Emergency Medical Hotline – can we help you?*

BAD GIRL: Er, yes…just *supposing* my estranged husband was lying bleeding at my feet, could you help?

OPERATOR: *Sure. We would send around a state-registered nurse right away…*

BAD GIRL: Yes, but what if he was *really* bleeding. Like, buckets of the stuff.

OPERATOR: *Er, whereabouts?*

BAD GIRL: Ooh, let's pretend…below the neck, above the ribs, smack bang in the middle but a bit to the left.

OPERATOR: *Well, in that case we'd have to organize an ambulance to get him to intensive care for complete round-the-clock medical attention.*

BAD GIRL: (DISAPPOINTED) Oh. So I suppose that means – hypothetically, of course – that no-one could sneak down the hospital corridor, creep into his room and turn off his life-support system?

OPERATOR: *That's right. And we would also organize the full transferral of all his medical records from his local GP to the hospital.*

BAD GIRL: So everyone would realize that he's asthmatic, diabetic, allergic to penicillin and has high blood pressure as a result of marital stress?

OPERATOR: *(CHEERFULLY) That's right!*

BAD GIRL: (SEVERELY DISGRUNTLED) Oh, well. Thanks anyway. (HANGS UP PHONE ABRUPTLY)

HUNT IT DOWN AND KILL IT

Stalking for Beginners

Sometimes, just sometimes, petty revenge is simply not enough. Sometimes you want a man to *really* pay for what he's done to you. You want him to remember his crime until death. Oh, and you also don't want him to forget you. Or enjoy his freedom. Or be able to sleep at night. Or think his life is better without you. Or enjoy another (more successful) relationship.

If that's how you feel, then the only sensible solution is to act like a man. Start chasing the object of your desires. Do what he initially promised to do for you when romance was a blooming rose rather than a bleeding ulcer: follow him to the ends of the earth (and pay no heed to those reluctant police officers dragging their feet behind you).

Preparing for the Kill

As stalking is a full-time occupation, quit your job beforehand or at least ask your boss if you can do it on a freelance basis. Then, after you've bought all your camouflage clothes and have finished polishing your telescopic rifle, ring your family and friends and tell them you're going to be lying low for a while. If they ask you why, sob and sniff down the phone a little and say that your ex has started to act like a crazed loon so you're going into hiding. This blatant lie to potential character witnesses could set up a strong case in your defence should you ever, perish the thought, end up on murder charges.

Marking Your Territory

Start off small. Use your previous extensive knowledge of his daily routine to pre-empt his movements, spoil his day and prevent him from accusing you of following him. Hop on the bus the stop before his. Jump the queue that he's in at the bank. Get down to his local pub before he does. Then start making sinister appearances in unusual places at odd times to unhinge him even more. For instance, turning up outside the men's toilet door of his local pub at ten o'clock at night should rattle him nicely, particularly if your telescopic rifle doesn't fit that snugly under your flak jacket.

Making It Legal

If you're stalking your prey properly, the first thing he'll do is go to the magistrate's court and get a restraining order put out on you. Once, he couldn't bear you out of his sights – now he wants you so many feet away from him, you'd be hard-pressed to see him, let alone shoot him. Fine. If he wants to be like that, then let him. But not before going on the counterattack by issuing him with a restraining order too. That way, you both have to appear in court together (the only legal time you'll be allowed in his presence from now on) and he'll end up with a criminal record as well as you.

Ignoring Restraining Orders

Restraining orders – like the promises of lying, two-faced, cheating, scumbag ex-lovers – were made to be broken. In fact, the idea that your ex has had the audacity to stoop so low as to fraternize with low-life solicitors will inevitably whip you up into an even more froth-like frenzy. Now it's war. Now it's not just letting his car tyres down, it's nipping the brake cable while you're at it. Now it's not just bursting into his bedroom unannounced and begging him to come back, it's bursting out of his closet with half-a-dozen slashed suits over your arm. At this stage, even the neighbours are starting to complain. And as for his new girlfriend, well, she left ages ago; about the same time as you burst into his bedroom and kicked her out.

Avoiding Police Interference

This is a fairly simple task since the police are notoriously reluctant to get involved in domestic disputes of any kind. Unless your victim is Brad Pitt or your stalking techniques are so good that you have managed to actually trip over your ex, set your rifle off and cause fatal head injuries in the process, you're not likely to be bothered by the boys in blue. And, even if you are, you can always bluff your way out of an arrest by saying your ex was harassing *you* which, when you think about it, is a lot easier to believe – especially if you managed to break your heel during the unfortunate shooting mishap on the pavement.

Quitting While He's Still Ahead

If, during stalking duties, your shoes are beginning to pinch, or you discover that you can't reload and fire your rifle, and hold your handbag at the same time, it may be time to abandon the chase. Give up, go home, soak your feet in one of those electric pedicure-spa things and wait, rifle at hand...because, as every girl knows, affecting sudden and massive disinterest in your ex is sure to trigger the inevitable. The awkward bastard's bound to start chasing you again.

Author's Note: As the sheer volume of women on Valium, in refuges, under police protection or out of the country will attest, stalking is still a mainly male pass-time. This is not to say, however, that we girls aren't capable of suddenly skidding to a halt, executing a half-turn, facing our demons and then pursuing them to hell and back. It's just that we don't like to look as idiotic as them.

Rude Retort

If a man starts to tell you he needs some space, tell him to go and join NASA.

YOU CHARGE *HOW* MUCH?

Legal Advice For Women With Marital Problems

Money matters might be the biggest cause of arguments during a long-term relationship, but that's nothing compared to the ferocious fiscal feuds that can occur before and after one. And, despite all those divorced men who like whinging/boasting to their new girlfriends about how much money they had to hand over to their previous wives, women on the whole tend to come out of the deal a lot poorer than men do. To redress the balance a little, and to save you getting a bum-steer from by-the-book solicitors, here's some free alternative advice for a broad range of financial grievances.

My rich fiancé has postponed our wedding because he thinks I'm just marrying him for his money even though I have assured him I am not. How else can I put his mind to rest?

Tell him you'll sign a pre-nuptial agreement. Better still, insist upon signing a pre-nuptial agreement. He'll then rest assured that your motives are pure and your intentions are good. In fact, he'll be so ashamed of doubting you, he'll refuse to let you sign it. Sucker.

My millionaire partner won't marry me until I sign a pre-nuptial agreement. I'd be happy to do so except that I don't think contracts are very romantic. However, I am keen to tie the knot because my partner's rather unwell at the moment and I want to be a dutiful wife during his last dying hours.

I sincerely hope you read this in time. For God's sake, sign the pre-nup. But, before you do, quietly nip down to your doctor's, affect a nervous breakdown and get yourself a medical certificate. Then, if you find out your husband is likely to make a full and permanent recovery, you can render the contract you signed null and void with written proof that you were not of sound mind when you entered into it.

I have been living with my boyfriend for 12 years and now he wants us to break up. Is it true I am not automatically entitled to half the furniture?

Alas, in the eyes of the law, a *de facto* relationship is not held in quite the same regard as a marriage. I suggest you take your half of the furniture without his permission, preferably while he's out.

I am a mother and a housewife who does not work, mainly because my husband won't let me. What I want to know is this: is it against the law to siphon money from our joint bank account into my own secret personal one – just in case I need emergency funds should I ever wish to leave him and the kids?

Unfortunately, your dilemma is one concerning morals and ethics rather than legalities. All I can say to assuage your conscience is that you're probably not doing anything your husband hasn't been doing already.

My husband has left me and our five young children for another woman. The kids and I still live in the family home but he is refusing to pay the mortgage, saying he can't afford that *and* romantic weekends with his new girlfriend in the South of France. How can I make him meet his financial responsibilities?

Shower and dress the kids, pack their overnight bags and take them over to his and her new place on a weeknight. Drop them off and tell him that they're all his — for good. The mortgage payment for the house will be in your bank account faster than you can take it out again to splurge on a haircut, a make-over and a subscription to the gym.

I have been married four times and each time has proved to be a bitter disappointment. All four of my husbands turned out to be lazy, selfish, boorish, childish and deceitful, and all of them left me for other women — though not before cleaning out all my life savings each and every time. Am I gay?

Gay? No. A hopeless romantic? Yes.

Prayer for the Day

If you want to leave a relationship with as much money as possible yet do not wish to be responsible for your partner's death, put your hands together and hope that he gets accidentally run over by a negligent, fully-insured lorry driver.

3

FAME,
FORTUNE & BLOODY
HARD WORK

3.1 JOB HUNTING WITH A CARVING KNIFE

*"Lack of education is an extraordinary handicap
when one is being offensive."*
Josephine Tey

International body-counters reveal that females comprise one-third of the world's official workforce but manage to clock up two-thirds of the world's work hours. Well, some of them do. Some girls – the good ones probably – might spend long and tiring days working for low wages and lousy bosses. Other girls – the bad ones, definitely – spend a relatively pleasant seven-and-a-half hours chatting, smoking, shopping, eating and drinking while waiting to be talent-spotted by a Hollywood casting agent or an old, rich and ailing man.

However, while life's only real purpose is to serve as a conduit to huge fame and great fortune, most girls – even the bad ones – have to start from more humble beginnings. They have to get a job. Then they have to go to work and be seen to be working. Occasionally, at least.

So, to help you on your way toward the bright lights and big money, here's an extensive guide to courses for reluctant students, plus advice on how to land a dream job with as little effort or education as possible. Oh, and there are also some handy tips about dodging the DSS, outwitting the tax man and suing people for fun and profit.

Student Advice
Instead of worrying about making student loan repayments, why not ask your parents for the money?

THE PAPER SHREDDER ATE MY HOMEWORK

Compulsory Courses For Reluctant Students

Art, Craft & Design
- How to Remove Felt-Tip Pen Marks From Clothes.
- Car-Key Calligraphy For Scorned Women.
- Pottery Throwing (How To Mend It Afterwards optional).

Business & Management
- Tax Evasion – Beginners Class.
- Tax Evasion – Intermediate Class.
- Tax Evasion – Advanced Class.

Computer & Office Skills
- How to Switch On A Computer.
- Two-Finger Typing In One Easy Lesson.
- Fixing Paper Jams In Printers.

English Language & Literature
- Learning To Speed-Read Boring Books.
- Understanding Plays Written By Dead Bards.
- Avoiding Library Fines By Avoiding Libraries.

Fashion & Beauty

- Design Your Own Comfortable G-String.
- Applying Cosmetics While Driving A Car.
- Hair Dying Kits And How To Use Them Properly.

Food & Drink

- How To Clean Sandwich Makers.
- Ordering Home Delivery Made Quick And Efficient.
- Basic Drinking Skills.

Foreign Languages

- Swearing In French.
- Shouting In Italian.
- Whispering In War-Torn Countries.

Health & Complementary Therapies

- Curing Hangovers With Painkillers.
- Yoga For Women Who Aren't Double-Jointed.
- Eating Muesli Made Fun.

Home, Car & DIY

- How to Hang Towels Up In Your Bathroom.
- 1001 Things to Do While You Wait For The Mobile Car-Repair Man.
- How To Get Someone Else To Assemble Your Self-Assembly Furniture.

Humanities & Social Sciences
- Tracing Madness And Neurosis Back To Your Ancestors.
- Map Reading Skills To Pass On To Mini Cab Drivers.
- Philosophy For Girls In Armchairs.

Media
- Writing Rubbish And Getting It Published.
- Selling Stories To *The National Enquirer.*
- Extracting Money From Excitable Nerds On The Net.

Music, Dance & Drama
- Learning To Appreciate Jazz Music By Switching It Off.
- Treating Corns, Bunions, Torn Muscles And Crippled Legs.
- How To Act Like A Drama Queen And Get Paid For It.

Science & Technology
- Genetic Engineering For Discerning Mothers.
- Understanding Instruction Manuals.
- Suing Your Cosmetic Surgeon For Botching Things Up.

Sport & Fitness
- Coping with Grief And Loss During The Football Season.
- Doing Aerobics Without Getting Fat Calf Muscles.
- Low Intensity Breathing Exercises.

Teaching & Childcare

- Basic Training In Corporal Punishment.
- Effective Cures For Nits, Worms And Scabies.
- Interviewing Nannies Made Easy.

Travel & Tourism

- Getting Plane Upgrades Without Having To Be Nice To Ground Staff.
- Looking Less Guilty When Going Through Customs.
- Self-Diagnostic Techniques In Third World Countries.

Study Note

If you live in a house-share or flat-share situation, night classes are a great way of missing your turn to cook dinner, whereas week-end courses are perfect if you want to avoid your share of household cleaning duties.

WHEN I GROW UP I WANT TO BE A CAUSE OF HUMAN SUFFERING

The A-Z of Jobs For Girls Behaving Badly

A

Accountant You can stop small talk at dinner parties simply by revealing what you do for a living.

Actor You can lie for a living.

Acupuncturist You can stick pins into people you dislike.

Air Traffic Controller You can send tourists on detours.

Ambulance Driver You can drive over the speed limit.

Anthropologist You can snoop through people's bathroom cabinets.

Archaeologist You can dig up people's flower beds.

Architect You can design buildings that people have to live in.

Art Gallery Owner You can sneer at all your customers.

Artist You can make a lot of money with just a set of crayons, a blindfold and one hand tied behind your back.

B

Baker You can bake bread past its use-by-date two minutes after it comes out of the oven.

Ballet Dancer You can retire early.

Banker You can charge people money for giving you their money.

Barrister You can take clients to the High Court if they don't pay their bills.

Bartender You can ignore all your customers.

Beautician You can tell other girls off for not using the right moisturizer.

Biochemist You can develop new drugs that cause really terrible side effects.

Bookmaker You can afford to buy your daughter a pony for Christmas.

Bookseller You can refuse to stock books by Barbara Cartland.

Bouncer You can beat up intellectuals.

Broadcast Engineer You can delay fixing transmission breakdowns during sports programmes.

Building Surveyor You can get paid to inform home-owners that their homes have dry rot, rising damp and subsidence.

Bus Driver You can brake suddenly.

Butcher You can tease vegetarians.

C

Cabin Crew Member You can leave the dining trolley in the aisle.

Careers Officer You can mislead students (see *Civil Servant*).

Carpenter You can make furniture that falls to pieces.

Casting Agent You can choose who you want to sleep with.

Chauffeur You can pretend you own the car that you're driving.

Chef You can hurl cutlery and steaming plates of food at apprentices.

Chiropodist You can tut-tut at the state of people's feet.

Chiropractor You can hurt people with back problems.

Choreographer You can make grown men wear tights.

Civil Servant You can kill the boredom of your job by dreaming up ways of murdering the person who persuaded you to take it in the first place (See *Careers Officer*).

Columnist You can slag off anyone you dislike in an amusing and witty way.

Hospital Porter You can spread germs.
Hotel Reservations Manager You can look blankly at people when they say their travel agent has already pre-booked.
Housekeeper You can forget to replace hotel guests' complimentary soaps, shampoos and shower gels.

I

Illustrator You can draw painstakingly life-like pictures to piss off photographers.
Information Officer You can be unhelpful wherever and whenever possible.
Insurance Agent You can convince customers to give you money for nothing.
Interior Designer You can convince clients that cork tiles are attractive.
Interpreter You can get a job on Miss World and improve upon their answers.

J

Jeweller You can sell items for thousands of pounds and then buy then back for a pittance.
Jockey You can make shortness of stature seem like an asset.
Journalist You can drink before lunch-time.

K

Kitchen Hand You can scrape all the left-overs into the bain-marie.

L

Laboratory Technician You can swap samples and change people's lives forever.

Lap Dancer You can tell all your girlfriends that men are a bunch of sad bastards.

Lecturer You can sleep with your students.

Legal Secretary You can understand all the small print in your work contract.

Literary Agent You can take 15 per cent commission for someone else's suffering.

Lorry Driver You can change lanes without bothering to check your front rear-view mirror.

M

Magazine Editor You can write the Editor's Letter and then go to lunch for the rest of the month.

Magician You can enjoy cutting your male assistant in half with a chainsaw.

Maintenance Person You can refuse to fix things properly.

Motorbike Courier You can cause cars to swerve when you pull out of a side street.

Make-up Artist You can forget your make-up bag.

Management Consultant You can charge enough to ensure that your opinion is valued.

Marine Biologist You can look at a seaweed health supplement without starting to retch.

Market Researcher You can interview lots of people and then state the blindingly obvious.

Masseur You can encourage lewd remarks at dinner parties by revealing what you do for a living.

Medical Secretary You can refuse to tell patients what is wrong with them over the phone.

Meteorologist You can forecast sunny periods.

Midwife You can smack very small children.

Milkman You can rattle crates loudly before 6am.

Milliner You can make women at white weddings look like fairground attractions.

Minicab Driver You can charge passengers whatever you feel like.

Model You can scowl, sulk or look bored on the job.

Motor Mechanic You can suck air through your teeth and shake your head.

Musician You can play cash-in-hand gigs five nights a week and collect unemployment benefits as well.

N

Nanny You can pretend to be a mummy without having to sleep with the daddy.

Naturopath You can encourage patients to take seaweed health supplements.

Newsreader You can smile at the misfortunes of others.

Nuclear Engineer You can clear crowded bars.

Nurse You can gain access to hard drugs.

O

Occupational Therapist You can get people back into the workplace well before they want to return.

Optician You can prescribe National Health Service glasses.

Optometrist You can diagnose eye laser surgery if you've run out of contact lens stocks.

Ordnance Surveyor You can miss out small streets on maps.

Osteopath You can *gently* hurt people with bad back problems (see *Chiropractor*).

P

Painter and Decorator You can leave work without having to clean up the mess you made.

Personal Assistant See *Secretary*.

Personnel Officer You can employ complete incompetents so you look good at your job.

Pest Controller You can kill insects, spiders, rodents and small family pets.

Pharmacist You can keep customers waiting for hours while you carefully tip five tablets into a bottle.

Physicist You can bore people rigid at dinner parties.

Piano Tuner You can make jazz pianists sound even worse.

Pilot You can hi-jack the plane.

Playwright You can write something nobody understands.

Plumber You can turn up for a job if, and when, you feel like it.

Poet You can become a journalist.

Police Officer You can run through red lights at intersections.

Politician See *Actor*.

Post Office Worker You can yawn or roll your eyes a lot when people ask for stamps.

Press Officer You can write government press releases that provide false or misleading information.

Printer You stop the press. Literally.

Probation Officer You can threaten people.

Proof Reader You can fail to spot a mistak.

Prostitute You can phone clients' wives up and demand compensation.

Psychologist You can play with people's minds.

Publican You can make Bourbon and Coke go further by serving it with ice.

Public Relations Officer You can get your teeth fixed and claim it as a tax deduction.

R

Railway Worker You can forget to show up at work and no-one will notice.

Receptionist You can be rude to couriers and callers alike.

Recruitment Consultant You can put up unsuitable candidates for unsuitable jobs.

Roadie You can sleep with groupies.

Roofer You can stamp your feet a lot.

Royal Photographer You can take pictures that nobody wants to look at.

Royal Biographer You can write books that nobody wants to read.

RSPCA Inspector You can pick up pets off the street and put them into a pound.

S

Salesperson You can smile insincerely.

Scaffolder You can sit on top of scaffolding and drink tea all day.

Sculptor You can make a lot of money with two nails, three bricks and a piece of chicken wire.

Secretary You can stop work until your boss starts referring to you by your proper job title (see *Personal Assistant*).

Security Guard You can stand or sit around doing nothing for long periods of time.

Shop Assistant You can hover around changing rooms without being arrested.

Singer You can get time off work just for having a sore throat.

Social Worker You can make people feel inadequate.

Soldier You can shoot foreigners.

Solicitor You can pretend you're a barrister.

Sport and Recreation Officer You can put people off going on another boat cruise.

Sportsperson You can get lucrative contracts with alcohol, soft drinks and fast food companies.

Stable Hand You can be excused for having bad breath.

Stage Hand You can be excused for feeling bitter.

Statistician You can fudge figures because no-one else is idiotic enough to want to double-check them.

Stockbroker You can earn lots of money without having to explain why.

Structural Engineer You can make bridges, banks and government buildings collapse.

Sub-Editor You can bitch about journalists' bad grammar.

T

Tailor You can snigger while measuring a man's inside leg.

Taxi Driver You can talk about politics and be guaranteed a captive audience.

Tax Consultant You can charge people for paying their tax bill.

Tax inspector You can pick on adults who are richer than you.

Teacher You can pick on kids who are cleverer than you.

Telecommunications Operator You can refuse to pick up the phone.

Tour Operator You can go bust.

Traffic Warden You can fine customers for abusing you.

Train Driver You can take long lunches while your train is being fixed.

Travel Agent You can forget to book flights and make reservations.

U

Undertaker You can wear black every day to the office.

V

Veterinary Nurse You can honestly say that your job stinks.

Veterinary Surgeon You can charge money for putting people's pets down.

W

Waitress You can serve up meals that people didn't ask for.

Wedding Photographer You can take pictures that nobody but the immediate family want to look at.

Window Dresser You can put nothing in the window and call it art.

Wine Merchant You can drink 20 times more than anyone else because you don't have to pay retail prices.

Wine Taster You can drink for a living.

Writer You can go totally mad and nobody will notice the difference.

Y

Youth Worker You can play pool during working hours.

Z

Zoo Keeper You can frighten visitors by leaving the cages unlocked.

Handy Hint

Always send your resumé out to prospective employers on very brightly-coloured paper. That way, the cleaners can spot it easily when they come to empty the wastepaper bins.

MINION...MANAGER...WHAT'S THE DIFFERENCE?

Rewriting History For The Sake of Prosperity

A standard but extremely creative resumé should always take the following details into account:

Personal Details

- Do give your name, address and work telephone number when writing your CV.
- Do not give your social security or parole number. (Also, for security purposes, do not give your Visa card number, your daily bank account transaction card PIN or your mother's maiden name).
- Do not disclose your date of birth unless you want to be immediately written off as too overqualified or too underqualified for the job.
- Do not disclose your current salary or otherwise you will have nothing to lie or argue about during your interview with your potential employer.
- Do not reveal your star sign.
- To avoid job discrimination do not attach a passport photograph of yourself. Portrait-size, full-colour, professionally airbrushed pictures are far more flattering and therefore much more likely to get you an interview.

Special Interests

It is perfectly acceptable to stretch the truth a little because most employers won't want to socialize with you after hours – especially if you disclose what you, supposedly, like to do in them. For instance, if your real hobbies are drinking, smoking, shopping and sex, list your special interests as reading, painting, playing chess and listening to Mozart.

Education

Unless you have spent time in prison and have therefore had easy access to free education, list as many diplomas, degrees and PhDs as you haven't got. Few employers – particularly those in the medical, teaching, legal and postal services – bother to check up on academic credentials anyway.

Job Title

Always embellish. Therefore wages clerk becomes *Financial Director*; general dogsbody becomes *Office Manager*, and office secretary becomes *Personal Assistant*.

Job Description

Always elaborate: you don't just type letters all day, you type them neatly, quickly and without making complaints; you don't just make tea for other staff members, you do it without slopping milk in the saucer; you don't just do the staff payrolls at the end of the month, you do them without ever once cocking up.

Duration of Job

Even if you haven't managed to keep any previous job for more than a year, you will still have to pretend that you have. Getting your facts right shouldn't prove too logistical a nightmare since it is assumed that while fine-tuning your resumé, you will be doctoring your references as well. (NB Any long periods of unemployment can always be explained away with the impressive but essentially meaningless phrase, *Travelled Overseas*.)

Reasons for Leaving

Good reasons include:

- To further my career.

Bad, though probably valid, reasons include:

- To get paid more.
- To get to sleep in more.
- To serve time in jail for firebombing my previous place of employment.

References

Never attach references to your resumé or prospective employers, with a keen eye for detail and too much time on their hands, may notice that all the letters are typed in the same font, using the same paper and bearing the same left-handed, sloping-to-the-right looped signature. Instead, write *References supplied upon request*. You can then always pull them out of your briefcase at the end of the interview when your prospective employer is looking anxiously at his watch and wondering whether he's missed the tee-off at the golf course.

Rewriting Job references

To whom it may concern

During the time she worked in my employ, this employee was extremely hardworking, punctual, loyal, honest, enthusiastic and talented. Unfortunately I had to get rid of her because I started to feel threatened.

To whom it may concern

During the time she worked in my employ, this employee was extremely hardworking, punctual, loyal, honest, enthusiastic and talented. Unfortunately I had to get rid of her because she did not fit in with this company's work philosophy.

To whom it may concern

During the time she worked in my employ, this employee was extremely hardworking, punctual, loyal, honest, enthusiastic and talented. Unfortunately I had to get rid of her because I failed to notice these qualities, having being out on the golf course for the last 18 months.

To whom it may concern

During the time she worked in my employ, this employee was extremely hardworking, punctual, loyal, honest, enthusiastic and talented. Unfortunately I had to get rid of her because she asked for a pay rise.

How to behave if you do want the job

1. *If your prospective employer's secretary/personal assistant asks if you would like a coffee, get on her good side by politely refusing, thus increasing your chances of being hired.*

2. *Upon introduction, take care to shake your interviewer's hands to rid yourself of sweaty palms.*

3. *Look the interviewer directly in the eye at all times so you can unnerve him into giving you a job.*

4. *Always pause before answering a question to give yourself ample time to make up a convincing lie.*

5. *Never ask how much the job pays, or you might be tempted to walk out before the interview ends.*

6. *Appear interested in the dealings of the company and its staff — even if you're not. Ask the interviewer pertinent questions such as what your job description is, who at the office is shagging who, and when was the last time the company got into trouble with its taxes?*

What to say if you don't want the job

Personnel Officer	*So, er, what made you apply for this job?*
Bad Girl	(SULLENLY) The Department of Social Security.
Personnel Officer	*Sorry?*
Bad Girl	You don't get your benefits if you're not seen to be looking for work.
Personnel Officer	*Oh, I see. So, why do you want this job?*
Bad Girl	Because I don't want to go on another bloody government training scheme.
Personnel Officer	*What do you think you can offer this company?*
Bad Girl	Tax relief and salary contributions from the government.
Personnel Officer	*Ahem. Okay then. What are your greatest strengths?*
Bad Girl	I'm young, fit, able-bodied and capable of achieving anything.
Personnel Officer	*And your biggest flaw?*
Bad Girl	I don't like working.

3.2 YOU DON'T HAVE TO BE STUPID TO WORK HERE...

"There was a time when certain people wanted to put me in jail. Now they've gone to jail and I'm still working."
Jane Fonda

Panic-stricken men, fuelled by misleading statistics, are claiming that females are taking over the workplace. Over-running it, maybe. But taking over? True, more and more girls are choosing to enter the work-force as an option that's better than staying at home. However, what those poor, masculine dears fail to mention in their overwrought arguments, during hysterical hand-wringing sessions, is that this so-called feminization of what used to be strictly a man's world, is found mostly in low-status service-industry jobs offering appalling pay and outrageous working conditions. Not the piddling 24-foot corner office on the top floor of a Fortune 500 company for us female firebrands. No, siree. Employers are begging us to toil in their eminently more enticing factories, and shops and cafés and broom closets the size of a secretary's work-station. And the only reason we're being bombarded with such job offers is because we don't nag or whine or moan or complain – unlike one half of the human race mentioned here.

Well, it's about time some girl changed all that. It's about time some girl pointed out the foibles and failings of utterly crap jobs for totally crap money. It's about time some girl dished the dirt on bastard bosses and unfriendly work-mates. And, hell, it might as well be you. Go on. Arm yourself with the following working girl's manifesto, show the lot of them who's boss and *really* start taking over the workplace.

PLEASE SIR, CAN I HAVE SOME MORE MONEY?

How To Exploit Your Bastard Boss

It is worth pointing out at this stage that I have used the highly sexist term "he" when referring to the bastard men who get paid for making your life hell. This is only because the people in the top jobs are most likely to be men* which in turn means they're likely to be bastards.

The Egomaniacal Bastard Boss

This one is usually found sitting behind the office door marked "King of the World and Emperor of All Others" because he can't actually get his head through it. Too wrapped up in his own brilliance to consider yours, the god-like figure you prefer to call "that pompous wanker" will only deign to consider your presence if you meekly knock on the door, humbly bow before him and ask him to tell you again about the time he fought and won both World Wars all by himself. This usually gives you four hours grace before you have to go back to your desk to work.

How to get a pay rise Forge a company letter outlining the details of your new and improved salary. Then trot off to his shrine, knock politely at the door and shyly say "Can you sign this please?" He, quite naturally thinking you're asking for his autograph, will do so.

How to get a promotion Dribble. Stutter. Twitch. Chop off a leg and get a rash. He'll promote you immediately now there's no chance you'll outshine him.

Unless, of course, you happen to work in a brothel or a convent.

The Bullying Bastard Boss

Post-It notes and biros aren't the only things that go missing round the office under this despot's regime. Your hearing also tends to disappear whenever he catches you stealing the Post-It notes and biros. Nothing you can do or say will ever stop the ferocity of his attack, especially since you can't actually do much with your arm twisted up around your back nor say much when he's yelling down your ear. And it doesn't help when there's an audience of cowering but secretly crowing colleagues silently encouraging him on – they're not the one who's going to have to wear an unsightly hearing aid for the next month.

How to get a pay rise Discard your hearing aid. Buy a set of earplugs. Practise wincing. Then go and ask him for your pay rise and don't back down until he's shouted and screamed himself to death.

How to get a promotion Ask his successor for one as soon as soon as your ears have stopped ringing.

The Sleazy Bastard Boss

Hah. The only chance he'll get horizontal with you is when you lay him out on the staff room floor for trying to touch your backside while you were bending over. Use you well-honed diplomatic skills and tactfully give him the brush off ("Get lost, pervert" should do nicely). Once this little misunderstanding is cleared up and he's gone back to his peep-hole above the girls' toilet you can get back to more important tasks, like painting your toenails.

How to get a pay rise Easy. Wear the shortest of skirts, the highest of heels and the see-throughiest of blouses to work. Then brush past him as you get up out of your office chair to make your way to his office to ask him for one.

How to get a promotion Wearing exactly the same items of clothing, wait until he chooses to promote, above you, another more conservatively-dressed female colleague. Then threaten to sue him for sex discrimination.

The Cheap-Skate Bastard Boss

If you're still banging away at a Tomasetti typewriter and sending faxes by Telex machine, then you've landed yourself a tight-wad boss – and don't let him tell you otherwise. Yes, it could be seen as a charming gesture to old-fashioned moral values and a thumb-on-the-nose to the evils of twenty-first-century-technology. It could also be seen as the penny-pinching ways of the same bastard who, when he catches you unfurling a paperclip because you're bored, makes you furl it back up again.

How to get a pay rise Forget it. Just start stealing expensive antiques from the office, or museum-standard machinery from the factory and do what everyone else does when things go missing round the work place: blame it on the cleaners.

How to get a promotion Apply for the newly created "Security Officer" position within the company. The pay will still suck, the hours will still stink but, apparently pre-World War I binoculars can sell for a fortune on the black market.

The Know-It-All Bastard Boss

Unable to let you do anything without his expert opinion and hovering presence, this bastard boss will have you wishing there was a law against being put into jail for killing someone with cold-blooded intent. Whether you're a highly-skilled surgeon or a fully-trained dish-washer, he'll never let you alone. He'll breathe down your neck while you're washing sharp implements. He'll show you the correct way to don rubber gloves. And, with a bit of luck, he'll also tell you how to sever his jugular vein without getting blood on the walls.

How to get a pay rise Unfortunately, the annual minimum wage increase does not apply within the penitentiary system.

How to get a promotion Start worrying about more relevant issues like how to get parole.

The Anally-Retentive Bastard Boss

This nit-picking pettifogging nerd would test the patience of a saint, let alone a sinner. Indeed, you will often feel the inexplicable and sudden desire to lose your temper and brain him with your counting machine whenever he's in the same room as you – which happens to be a lot since he's always checking up on you to check you're checking the figures that three junior employees have already individually checked after the weekly stationery stock-take was done.

How to get a pay rise Race into his office, and through excited gulps of breath, tell him you've at last spotted an error in some of the company's figures. After telling you to rectify the mistake at once, he'll be so chuffed he's finally found a kindred spirit, he'll probably not bother to check and find out that the error is in your salary.

How to get a promotion Ironically, thanks to your newfound attention to petty and mind-numbingly boring details, you'll be promoted – willingly or not – to Chief Checker of the Senior Checker Checking the Junior Checkers Immediately Following The Weekly Stationery Stock-Take.

The Phantom Bastard Boss

In an ideal world, the boss who is never around would be an ideal boss. Unfortunately, the absent employer tends to cause more misery and mayhem out of your sight than if he were to sit in the middle of your desk and dribble coffee into your hard drive for eight hours. This is mainly because while he's off jetting about the world's greatest golf courses on Very Important Business, there never seems to be anybody senior enough at the office to sign important documents like your expense sheets or pay cheques.

How to get a pay rise A more pressing issue, perhaps, than how to get a pay rise might be working out how to get *paid*.

How to get a promotion You can't even console yourself with a more hallowed position in the company, since you've got to be singled out by your boss for greatness. And he's hardly going to be able to do that when he's "Having A Meeting" on the ninth hole in Haiti now, is he?

Unemployment Benefit
Charging your employer with sexual harassment, falsely or not, is a great way to ensure that you never get employed again.

WHO'S TAKEN MY STAPLER AGAIN?

Why All Work Colleagues Should Be Sackable Offences

When push comes to shove, mean, petty and small-minded colleagues are not that much different from mean, petty and small-minded bosses. Indeed, colleagues are probably worse because they have to work alongside you without the kickbacks, bonuses and other bribes your boss gets for his pains. Whether it's brothers-up-in-arms-about-you-using-their-tea-mugs or comrades-at-war-with-you-for-stealing-their-staplers, there are only two options for dealing with whining work-mates. One is to beat them at their own game using the following crash course in pro-active passive aggressiveness. The second is to ignore all the advice given and, instead, plan how to use your time in prison in a positive and useful way.

Day-To-Day Politics

- Stop colleagues stealing chocolate bars and potato snacks by using sticky tape to secure them to the underside of your desk.
- Hide in the toilets when it's your turn to make tea for your work-mates.
- Fall out with a colleague who's leaving so you don't have to contribute money to his or her going-away gift.

Successful Gossip-Mongering

- Sit quietly on the toilet in the girls' room for five minutes at the beginning, the middle and the end of work.
- Tell the receptionist what you heard in the toilets – then go to your desk and wait.
- Drop a quiet word in the ear of the devastated victim and tell her you know who was responsible for spreading the gossip around the entire office but you'll only tell her it was the receptionist if she promises to keep it a secret.

Games of Petty One-Upmanship

- Leave your wage slip in full view of anyone who gets paid less than you.
- Talk loudly down the phone to your accountant about your pay increase within earshot of anyone who didn't get one.
- Get a loved one to send huge bouquets of flowers to you at your office – even when it's not Valentine's Day.

Basic Back-Stabbing Etiquette

- Bitch about colleagues who are on leave, off sick or out of the room.
- Act non-committal when a boss asks you your honest opinion of an absent colleague's performance at work.
- Act non-committal when your boss praises an absent colleague's work in front of you.

Effective Non-Confrontational Techniques

- Refuse to look at, talk to or work with a colleague who has unwittingly slighted you.
- Tell all other work colleagues about one colleague's crimes.
- Borrow the culprit's stapler when he or she isn't looking, and secretly return it later without bothering to refill it.

Small Business Tip

To make extra money while working full-time, why not take up a telemarketing job using your phone at the office.

CAN YOU SIGN MY EXPENSE FORMS?

Thwarting And Ripping Off The System From Within

During work hours

- Get into the habit of making and taking all personal phone calls between the hours of 9am to 5pm on weekdays only.
- Redirect all business calls to your office voice-mail and only call people back if it's urgent and they've called you at least three times already.
- Cut down on hours actually worked by attending, or calling, more meetings.
- Cut down on hours actually worked by taking lots and lots of cigarette breaks.

During lunch hours

- Capitalize upon temporary office down-time by using the colour photocopier and the fax machine to make and then send personal party invitations to 500 of your closest friends.
- Take the finance department's embittered lackey to lunch, get her drunk, and find out how much everyone in the office is getting paid.
- Take a notebook and pen to the pub and bill the subsequent liquid lunch to your company as a working one.
- Eat a sandwich and read a magazine at your desk for an hour in the middle of the day and then leave work 60 minutes early in lieu of missing your lunch-break.

After hours

- On your way out of the office building, take vast supplies of stationery and as much office equipment as you can carry under the not-untruthful pretext that you're taking your work home with you.
- Work late at the office in order to type up your resumé and to produce a lavish full-colour, fully-bound, laminated work-presentation folder using office facilities, amenities and supplies.
- Work late at the office in order to make international, personal calls using those staff members' phones that, you know, don't have bars on them.
- Attend any work function held by your company and system-atically drink the bar dry.

SHORT DAY WEEKS AND LONG WEEKENDS

Good Enough Reasons To Skive Off Work

"I don't feel so good."

"I think it might have been the prawns I ate last night."

"I'm not very well."

"I've been throwing up all night."

"I've got flu."

"I think it might be a viral infection."

"My back's out."

"I've got RSI."

"I've got ME."

"I've got to go to the dentist."

"I'm having my wisdom teeth out."

"I haven't got any clean clothes to wear."

"My make-up bag's gone missing."

"I've lost a contact lens."

"My aunt's friend's cat's gone missing."

"My grandmother's just died again."

"I've got to go to a funeral."

"I've got women's problems."

"I've had a row with my boyfriend again."

"I've got a doctor's note."

"I've got another job interview."

"My washing machine's just flooded."

"I've got to wait for the plumber."

"I'm needed for jury duty."

"I'm stranded at the airport."

"I'm sick."

"I'm really sick."

"I'm dying."

"No, no. You don't understand, I'm really dying."

"I think I've got terminal cancer."

"Oh, alright then. I haven't. But I've got a really rotten hang-over."

Health Hint

When phoning in sick at work, add a little authenticity to your claim by hitting yourself lightly over the head with a steak mallet. Then while lying prone on the bed, place a handkerchief over the mouthpiece and make your call while speaking with a mouthful of dry muesli.

GET THAT DOG AWAY FROM ME

What to do when the honeymoon is over

So you've taken too many sickies and had too many long lunches. You've asked for and not got too many pay rises and you've left too many half-eaten yoghurts to rot in the staff kitchen's fridge. You've also upset too many people – particularly the boss who resents being called "a two-bit, tin-pot Fascist who couldn't run a small, fully-automated, robotic, manufacturing plant let alone a multi-national corporation." So now you and your personal belongings are being escorted out of the building by two beefy security guards and an Alsatian with a keen nose for the laptop you've got hidden under your coffee mug. Good. You've been trying to get sacked for months.

Resignations

Unless you've got a fabulous new job to go to, never resign. If you leave your place of employ voluntarily, you don't qualify for employment benefits immediately unless you've got a good excuse, and "I didn't like having to work" probably won't cut it with the Department of Social Security. You're just going to have to sit it out and wait for a redundancy package or behave even worse than usual and, hopefully, get the sack so you can start claiming unfair dismissal.

Redundancies

A redundancy is an employer's polite and generous way of saying that a) "You're useless at your job but I don't want you suing me for unfair dismissal," or b) "It is cheaper for me to pay you a huge amount of money to stay at home than to pay you to come to work." Either way, it can come as a devastating blow to your ego. The only option is to cheer yourself up by blowing your pay-out on lots of new clothes.

Sackings

Getting sacked is preferable to handing in your resignation or getting made redundant, mainly because you can collect unemployment benefit straight away. These days it's enormously hard to get sacked, particularly if you work in a government department. This means you're going to have to take some fairly drastic measures in order to get thrown out of your office for good. Petty pilfering and occasional sniping isn't enough. Better tactics include fraud, embezzlement, blackmail, sabotage, stealing, assault, murder, genocide and taking someone else's fax off the fax machine while it's still going through because you can't be bothered to wait to send yours.

Unfair Dismissals

This is what should instantly follow your ejection from the building. To avoid being sued by you for an extortionate amount of money, your ex-boss has to have a very good reason for sacking you. Even supposing you had managed to reduce his staff levels by half, thanks to a vodka bottle full of kerosene and a small burning rag, there may still be grounds for legal action. And, even if there isn't, your self-serving, money-grubbing solicitor is sure to tell you otherwise.

Bank Note

Money doesn't grow on trees – you can, however, often find it in a gullible man's wallet.

3.3 CHARGE IT TO TWIT-FACE OVER THERE

"I get so tired of listening to one million dollars here, one million dollars there. It's so petty."
Imelda Marcos

According to some alarming reports from the United Nations, women work more hours than men yet earn only a tenth of the world's income. Worse still, women own less than a hundredth of the world's property. It's hardly surprising then, that after a long look at their credit card statements and a quick glance at their overdrafts, some girls will resort to every trick in the book to collect enough money for the rent. And it's only fair that I provide a helping hand. So without further ado, here are some ideologically incorrect savings plans and get-rich-quick schemes for struggling minxes who want to get out of the red and bleed all those better-off blokes dry.

Chauvinist's Corner

On average, a woman earns 80 per cent of a man's annual salary. The rest she gets for doing nothing.

I CAN'T BE EXPECTED TO LIVE ON THAT!

A Good Case For Giving Bad Girls More Money

We girls might get paid less than your bog-average man but, purely by dint of being the fairer sex, we need at least twice as much money as a male to survive. Unlike most men, who can generally live off the smell of a cheap bottle of aftershave they scored from a girlfriend the Christmas before last, we need expensive eau de parfum at least six times a year. And that's just the start of our list of high-priced, feminine essentials.

Girls, in general, also need extra money for:

Tampons

Sanitary towels

Panty liners

Period painkillers

Contraceptives

Vaginal deodorant

Lip liner

Lipstick

Lip gloss

Base

Blusher

Translucent powder

Mascara

Eyeliner

Eye shadow

Cleanser

Moisturizer

Toner

Tweezers

Wax

Body lotion

Cellulite cream

Face masks

Nail polish

Nail polish remover

Bra

Petticoat

Tights

Hair brush

Hair dryer

Hair spray

Handbag

Mobile phone (for safety purposes)

Taxi fares (ditto)

Bad girls, in particular, need extra money for:

Evening primrose oil (for PMT)

Douching kit

Thrush tablets

Slimming tablets

Stomach pump

Suspender belt

Stockings

Handcuffs

Whip

Leather zip-up mask

Concealer

Eye whitener

Hair dye

Bleach

Acrylic nails

Breast enlargements

Liposuction

Kick-boxing classes

Can of mace (for safety purposes)

Ice pick (ditto)

Bear these expenses in mind tomorrow when you ask for a pay rise and your employer asks why you need such an astronomical figure, or this evening when you refuse to give your partner a blow-job because he still owes you money for the one you gave him the night before.

Charitable Donation

A great and legitimate way to make extra money is to have a baby and then try to sell it on to a childless couple in Hollywood.

THE FREE DRINKS AREN'T ON ME

A Brief Introduction To Guilt-Free Blagging

There's no such thing as a free lunch, except when:

- your boss is paying.
- your parents are paying.
- you're on your first date.
- you put a fly in your soup.
- you're a restaurant critic.

The best things in life are free, only when:

- your drug dealer dies suddenly and bequeaths you all his possessions.
- you're a tax auditor and house-guest on a rich but shady entrepreneur's yacht.
- you're a travel writer.
- you're a social smoker.
- you're friends with the barman.

Money isn't everything, especially when:

- you're not the one footing the bill for the meal.
- you're not the one dealing with rival drug gangs.
- you're not the one doling out the fags.
- you're not the one having to write all the travel features and restaurant reviews.
- You're a tax auditor and house-guest on a rich but shady entrepreneur's yacht.

171

> ### Astonishing Fact
> *When put in the mail, bills tend to travel faster to their destination than cheques.*

OF COURSE, I'LL EMPTY YOUR COLOSTOMY BAG

How To Marry Into Extremely Old Money

When you're young, beautiful, broke and just about to tie the knot with a 90-year-old oil tycoon in advanced stages of pleurisy, getting accused of marrying him solely for his money is very annoying and very, very predictable. Like you reasonably point out to his relatives in hushed tones so as not to disturb the master of the house while he lies wheezing in his iron lung, you're hardly going to marry a *poor* old-age-pensioner now are you? Anyway, you say, to console yourself after your in-laws storm off in a self-righteous huff, the stupid old bugger's got no-one but himself to blame if he ever finds out you're shagging the chauffeur and have plans to turn his country estate into a theme park. I mean, if you were paunchy, grizzled and bald, would you be dumb enough to think someone fancied you for your looks?

How to attract the attentions of an old, rich and ailing man

- Be young.
- Be poor.
- Be attractive.
- Be vibrant.
- Look the picture of health.
- Be very, very smart.
- Loiter on oil fields.
- Swim past oil rigs.
- Pretend to drown near cruise ships.
- Get a job on a cruise ship.
- Get a job as a live-in nurse.
- Hang around inside private nursing homes.
- Hang around on private country estates.
- Hang around outside private gentlemen's clubs.
- Hang around at funerals for other rich but dead old men.
- Pretend you don't mind changing colostomy bags.
- Pretend you don't mind pushing wheelchairs.
- Pretend you don't mind cutting his food up.
- Pretend you don't mind wiping his chin.
- Pretend you don't want diamonds and furs and trips on his yacht.
- Refuse to have sex until after you're married.

The five golden rules for gold-diggers

1. *Money spent on haircuts and facials is money well spent. Money spent upon elocution classes or lessons in social etiquette is not. Old, rich and ailing men don't care if you call the toilet a lavatory or if you hold your knife and fork the wrong way up. However, they can spot grey hairs and wrinkles a mile off.*

2. *Full penetrative sex before marriage is not an option when you're trying to frustrate your old, rich and ailing fiancé. Fortunately, full penetrative sex after the marriage is also highly unlikely.*

3. *At the wedding ceremony, always kneel down next to the wheelchair and put your arms lovingly around your old, rich and ailing groom's grotesquely hunched shoulders so that your head doesn't get cut out of the wedding snaps.*

4. *To ensure that your old, rich and ailing husband signs the new will that you've had drawn up by his solicitors at his expense, detach his drip, remove his iron lung, threaten to let down the tyres on his wheelchair and put a pen into his lifeless hand. Have the chauffeur you've been shagging standing by to act as a witness.*

5. *Never try to befriend your old, rich and now recently deceased husband's ex-wives or offspring – otherwise you'll feel guilty for kicking them out of their houses, repossessing their cars and cutting off their allowances after the will has been read.*

Rash Thought

Whatever you do, don't get too carried away and actually have a baby with an old, rich and incontinent millionaire – otherwise you'll be changing nappies morning, noon and night.

174

I HAVE GOT SOME SCRUPLES, YOU KNOW

Making Money Without Having To Marry A Geriatric

Some bad girls wouldn't marry for money even if you paid them. If that sounds like you then you may have to turn to some alternative profit-making schemes. Go for it. Just make sure they're all ethically, if not legally, correct. (NB Robbing bus-shelters, mugging babies, or selling drugs to dead people are all definite no-nos.)

Blackmail made easy

1. *Type up the note, preferably using your office computer during office hours.*

2. *Print it out, preferably using the office printer during office hours.*

3. *Deposit it into your victim's in-tray during a busy lunch hour.*

4. *Wait the requisite five minutes for the panicked response.*

5. *Accept sudden and substantial pay rise with surprise and gratitude.*

6. *Ring your head-hunter and tell her you've decided not to take the new job after all.*

Suing for fun and profit

- Sue international charity organizations if the underprivileged third world child you sponsor fails to improve his or her grades at school.
- Take your partner to court for breach of promising absolutely anything – ever.
- Slap a writ on manufacturers of anti-wrinkle cream for providing misleading information.
- Throw the book at libraries for never being open.
- Seek compensation from fashion designers for making you wear mid-calf length skirts.
- Charge all friends automatically with libel, slander and defamation of character.

Gambling techniques for winners

- Fill out a Lottery form and forget to get it processed.
- Play poker with an emotional friend.
- Buy a Scratch 'n' Win card from your local newsagent and give it to someone else as a birthday gift.
- Bet on a horse that racing experts don't think will win.
- Bet on the same horse that jockeys, trainers and horse-owners think will win.
- Press the "Refund" button at telephone boxes and on any vending machines.

Introduction to better bank manager management

- **Do** knock before barging into his office and throwing yourself at his feet.

- **Do** point out that you've been a loyal and valued customer for the last four-and-a-half months.

- **Do** tell him about your previously good credit record without mentioning the clothes stores in question.

- **Don't** prejudice him by revealing you're a single young female (wear a balaclava if necessary).

- **Don't** tell him what you really plan to spend the money on.

- **Don't** threaten to shoot him when he refuses to hand over the money, unless you're prepared to go through with it.

Ways to Dodge The Tax Man:

1. *Die.*

Savings Tip

Avoid feeling the pinch by ensuring you have some emergency funds at hand. Start now by regularly dropping money down the back of your couch.

3.4 I'M FAMOUS... WHO ARE YOU?

"Success didn't spoil me. I've always been insufferable."
Fran Lebowitz

Unreliable, shallow and bereft of scruples, moral fibre or sanity, bad girls are born to be stars. Unfortunately, since they also tend to be forgetful, lazy, and completely mad, they often have to reach fame's dizzy heights by attaching themselves to someone more famous or talented or hardworking or better looking. Either that or they'll resort to murdering their grandmother by accident and then pretending that it was a deliberately calculated career move, after they've signed the three-book deal during their time on remand.

And that's the great thing about fame really. While good girls get committed for crimes and misdemeanours, bad girls get punished with gruelling press schedules or relentless invitations to film premieres, catwalk collections and Buckingham Palace on OBE hand-out day.

Grooming Tip
Bad girls should always wear their very best underwear, just in case they happen to get run over by a bus full of photographers.

MY MOTHER USED TO LOCK ME IN A CUPBOARD

Are You Destined For fame?

Find out your own capacity for fame, notoriety, and psychotic behaviour simply by ticking any of the following that have applied, do apply, or you wish would apply, directly to you. Score one point for each.

❏ A parent who is famous.
❏ A difficult childhood.
❏ A mis-spent youth.
❏ A child born to you out of wedlock.
❏ A child given to you by a single mother.
❏ A drink problem.
❏ A drug problem.
❏ An eating disorder.
❏ A nose job.
❏ A face lift.
❏ Liposuction.
❏ A nervous disposition.
❏ A nervous breakdown.
❏ Bad dress sense.
❏ Tendencies toward violence.
❏ An ability to throw tantrums in public.
❏ Rumours of excessive sexual proclivities and/or deviations.
❏ Embarrassing family members.
❏ Nude photos of yourself published without your permission.
❏ Nude photos of yourself published with your permission.
❏ One or more Web Sites devoted to you, naked or not.
❏ A tempestuous on-off relationship with at least one famous man.

❏ At least one abortion.
❏ At least one marriage.
❏ At least one divorce.
❏ A shoplifting charge.
❏ An assault charge.
❏ A suicide attempt.
❏ A murder attempt.
__ **Total Score**

Now tick any of the following which also apply directly to you.
Score one point for each.
❏ A successful rehabilitation.
❏ A happy relationship with a parent.
❏ A happy relationship with a man.
❏ A refusal to go under the knife.
❏ An ability to sing, dance, act, paint, write, play a musical
  instrument or talk intelligently.
__ **Total Score**

Take all the points you gained from your second Total Score and
deduct them from your first Total Score. You now have your correct
Fame Quotient Figure. If you scored less than zero expect to live a life
of anonymous desperation. If you scored between one and 19, you
could be destined for fame. If you scored 20 points or more, you're
probably famous already.

Celebrity Profile

*When being photographed coming out of McDonald's restaurants,
keep your head down at all times so that no-one can see any
spots on your chin.*

I COULDN'T HAVE DONE THIS WITHOUT MY AGENT

Ways To Get Famous If You're Not Very Talented

- Marry a man who is famous.
- Marry a man who is famously rich.
- Take all your clothes off for Playboy.
- Take all your clothes off for a Hollywood movie.
- Become a game show hostess.
- Act on a soap.
- Make a record after acting on a soap.
- Become a cable channel presenter.
- Become a TV presenter.
- Become a disc jockey.
- Become a weather girl.
- Become a newsreader.

I'D LIKE TO THANK MY LAWYERS

Ways To Get Famous If You're Not Very Bright

- Kidnap someone.
- Hijack a plane.
- Assassinate a president.
- Have sex with a president.
- Have sex with a politician.
- Have sex with one of your students.
- Have sex with a priest.
- Date a footballer.
- Be a guest on the Jerry Springer Show.

I OWE IT ALL TO GOD

Ways To Get Famous If You're Not Very Beautiful

- Find a cure for cancer.
- Find a cure for AIDS.
- Find the Missing Link.
- Create world peace.
- Save the Amazon rainforests.
- Direct an award-winning film.
- Script an award-winning play.
- Write a masterpiece.
- Paint a masterpiece.
- Have a one-night stand with a rock star.
- Get your face fixed and *then* become a weathergirl.
- Be a guest on the Jerry Springer Show.

DON'T YOU KNOW WHO I AM?

How To Act Like A Diva Even When You Aren't One

- Demand service at restaurants.
- Order something that's not on the menu.
- Jump the queues at nightclubs.
- Wear sunglasses indoors.
- Hang up on telephone operators.
- Slap policemen – or shop assistants.
- Park in disabled parking spaces.
- Refuse to pack your own bags at the supermarket.
- Demand discounts whenever you buy things.

Star Quota

If you want to get famous in less than 15 minutes, have sex with all the members of a Premier League football team, one after the other and then spend the remaining moments left talking to the press about it.

Ten Signs That You're Already A Prima Donna

1. *You throw furniture out of hotel windows.*

2. *You make it on to the front page of newspapers every time you get involved in a drunken brawl.*

3. *You refuse to pay your bodyguard his wages unless he sleeps with you.*

4. *You join a religious cult.*

5. *You sack your agent/manager for gross ineptitude.*

6. *You get sacked by your agent/manager for gross ineptitude.*

7. *You walk off talk shows when presenters ask you questions about your love life.*

8. *You have an entourage of nannies.*

9. *You borrow clothes from famous designers and then won't give them back.*

10. *You receive hate mail and/or get stalked by crazed fans.*

A Day In The Life Of A Star Behaving Badly

1.00pm   Get woken up by the hotel bell-boy.

1.03pm   Kick him out of bed, drink six glasses of complimentary champagne and have quick shower.

1.10pm   Scan updated press clippings file in hotel room while hair and make-up people work their magic.

2.30pm   Meet fiancé at lawyer's office to sign pre-nuptial agreement, then meet helicopter on law firm's roof.

2.35pm   Pick up new complimentary dress from complimentary clothes designer.

2.45pm   Get married in a hush-hush ceremony in the middle of Times Square but postpone the honeymoon because of hectic work schedule.

3.15pm   Take helicopter back to lawyer's office again to renegotiate pending *Playboy* contract.

3.25pm   Take helicopter to recently raved-about restaurant next door to lawyer's office.

3.30pm   Order meal. Send it back. Use head waiter's mobile phone to ring nanny and instruct her to pick up new son from the adoption agency.

3.35pm   While waiting for complimentary bottle of vodka from very apologetic restaurant chef, scan the social pages in the late afternoon edition newspaper and spot a picture of new husband at his stag night in compromising position with plain-faced laptop dancer.

4.00pm   Take helicopter to lawyer's office yet again and draw up divorce papers.

4.30pm   Meet personal trainer back at hotel* and ask him for some Valium to calm nerves.

11pm   Wake up in private room in top hospital's psychiatric ward.

11.01pm Place emergency calls through to agent, manager, publicist, lawyer, clothes designer and nanny.

11.10pm Conduct heart-rending interview from deathbed wearing complimentary silk pyjamas and then pose for pictures with soon-to-be-motherless-again son.

*Subject unable to go home since she owns so many houses she can't remember any of the addresses.

Comforting Thought
If you can't serve as a good example you can always serve as a horrible warning.

GET OUT OF MY FACE, BOZO

Surrounding Yourself With The Right Kind of People

How well you cope with celebrity isn't just up to ever-faithful and fawning publicists, parents and media mutts. Equally, how much of a cock-up you make of your 15 minutes/days/years isn't solely the result of copious drugs, marriages and tax bills. It's partly to do with how well you treat the people closest to you.

What to do with all those annoying hangers-on

- Get them to carry your bags through customs.
- Get them to carry your baby through customs.
- Get them to carry your drugs through customs.
- Get them to take your picture if the press hasn't turned up.
- Get them to open doors for you.
- Get them to mix your drinks.
- Get them to fix you a snack.
- Get them to fix your hair.
- Get them to conceal your eye-bags.
- Get them to do all your fan mail correspondence.
- Get them to take the film out of a photographer's camera.
- Get them to beat up photographers.
- Get them to shoot stalking fans.
- Get them to look after your kids.
- Get them to have sex with your partner when you're too busy.
- Get them to take all the brown ones out of a packet of M&Ms.
- Get them to look for your contact lenses whenever and wherever you drop them.
- Get them to trash your hotel room.
- Get them to tidy it up again.
- Get them to work out how to use your VCR.
- Get them to say nice things to you.
- Get them to say nice things about you to the press.
- Get them to leak things about your enemies to the press.
- Get them to sign contracts promising not to tell anyone about what you get them to do.

What to do with all those annoying fans

- Get them to buy your records.
- Get them to go and see your films.
- Get them to buy your books.
- Get them to buy your mugs.
- Get them to buy your t-shirts.
- Get them to buy your doll.
- Get them to write letters of adoration when stations or studios hire you.
- Get them to write letters of condemnation when stations or studios fire you.
- Get them to scream and faint a lot when you make an appearance in public.
- Get them to buy you drinks.
- Get them to sleep with you.
- Get them to sell their story to *News of the World*.
- Get them to apologize afterwards by sending you expensive gifts.
- Get them to send you expensive drugs in desperation.
- Get them to sleep with you again.
- Get them to send you poison pen letters when you don't return their calls the following morning.
- Get them to wait outside your hotel in the pouring rain.
- Get them to threaten to kill you so you can justify the expense of a bodyguard.
- Get them to threaten to kill someone else to prove their undying love for you.
- Get them arrested.
- Get them to tell the press about it.
- Finally agree to give them your autograph.

Things to say to thwart a wannabe

"One bottle of Krug and a packet of nuts, please."

"Sorry, I don't sign autographs after hours."

"So tell me what you thought of my scene again?"

Things to say to crush an also-ran

"Sometimes I envy you your life."

"You're not missing a thing, believe me."

"One bottle of Krug and a packet of nuts, please."

Things to say to kill a has-been

"I used to really look up to you when I was a kid."

"Did this sort of thing often happen to you too?"

"One bottle of Krug and a packet of nuts, please."

Things to say to piss off one of your peers

"And you are...?"

"Gosh, you look so much smaller in real life."

"Could you sign this for my mum?"

Did You Know?

Greta Garbo is probably the only star ever who managed to stay famous by not speaking to the press.

"NO COMMENT"

Refusing To Talk To The Press Unless You're Allowed To Lie

As any of those toothsome trouble-shooters known as publicists will tell you, whether your star is on the rise or on the fall, it's imperative that you lie through your teeth in order to give your paying public a good laugh. From image control to damage control, here are a few clichés and wallops of cod to trot out whenever there's a hack writer around.

I don't date people in the industry	*I can't stand the competition.*
I don't see myself as a sex symbol	*My publicist reckons modesty is becoming.*
I don't diet or exercise	*I do a lot of coke instead.*
That's a deeply offensive question.	*Yes, I have had my breasts enlarged and a rib removed.*
I don't earn as much as is reported	*I earn a hell of a lot more.*
I really admire her work	*I cannot stand the woman herself.*
I'm deeply misunderstood	*Everyone thinks that I'm a bitch.*

*I could live without
the fame.*

*I'd curl up and die if no-one
asked for my autograph.*

We're just good friends

*We're shagging like rabbits
but don't want to go public b ecause
a) one of us won't commit
or b) one of us is married.*

*My partner and daughter
take first priority*

*Now that my partner's found out
about my affair on set, I don't have
any choice.*

The split was amicable

*We hate each other's guts but there's
alimony and the kids to take
into consideration.*

And so on.

How to stay in the spotlight

1. *Get thrown off a film set for doing too many drugs.*

2. *Refuse to talk to the broadsheets about it.*

3. *Lie, instead, and talk about an "exciting new project" that's currently in the pipeline.*

4. *Get fired from the soap for being crap at acting.*

5. *Refuse to talk to the tabloids about it.*

6. *Talk about your drug problem instead.*

7. *Have an affair with another star in rehab.*

8. *Send the pictures, anonymously, to the world's biggest news agencies.*

9. *Divorce your husband when he reads all about it.*

10. *Do a touching and brave "life will go on without him" ten-page spread in* Hello!

11. *Marry someone new – preferably someone famous but not the star you had the affair with in rehab as that's already old news.*

12. *Give* Hello! *the exclusive rights to your wedding photographs.*

13. *Talk to* Okay *on your honeymoon and say how much you'd like a role in a film.*

14. *Start the whole cycle all over again.*

Famous Last Words

Fame is one of the very few instances where a girl can behave really badly and get away with it.

4

HOME, HEARTH & NOT-SO-HAPPY HOLIDAYS

4.1 SUPERWOMAN OR SUPERSLACKER?

"I hate housework! You make the beds, you do the dishes – and six months later you have to start all over again."
Joan Rivers

Turning a house into a home is never a bad girl's strong point. Too many painful flashbacks of pink frills around window frames and teddy bears artfully strewn on broderie anglais duvets send her screaming towards low-maintenance surrounds. Too many bygone barked orders to make her bed, dust her dressing table and help make the stuffing for the Christmas dinner have turned her into a right domestic rebel. A *bona fide* bad girl instinctively knows that life's far too short to stuff a button mushroom let alone a 20lb turkey. Indeed, a home-cooked meal is a contradiction in terms. And asking her what she thinks about housework is like asking a lettuce what it thinks about slugs.

So, until scientists invent ride-on vacuum cleaners and self-cleaning ovens, and until she can afford to pay some other sucker to do all her dirty work, a bad girl usually has to live in a dump.

Things you will never see in a bad girl's house

- Coffee table books on the coffee table.
- Socks in sock drawers.
- Toilet roll paper in the toilet.
- Cutlery in cutlery drawers.
- Clean mugs.
- Dry bath towels.
- Stain-free carpets.
- Dust-free Venetian blinds.
- Mould-free bathrooms.
- Empty ash-trays.
- Matching saucepans.
- Thriving pot plants.
- Flowers in proper vases.
- Freshly baked bread.
- Newly painted walls.
- A vacuum cleaner.
- A feather duster.
- An ironing board.
- A tea towel.
- A 20lb turkey.

Budget-Buster

If you're trying to dine out on a budget and you live in a residential area near to a motorway, road kill is always a cheap and nutritious option – and it's usually been filleted for you.

YOU WON'T EVEN NOTICE I'M HERE

How To Live Well At Someone Else's Expense

1. **Squatting** *Excellent idea if you're broke and you're fairly laid-back about your surrounds or you simply want to deter friends from dropping around on the weekend.*

2. **Staying with a friend** *A viable option if you've still got one and don't care if you haven't even got that one by the end of your prolonged and protracted stay.*

3. **House-minding** *A very cheap way to live in a very nice house. Providing, that is, you can actually get into the bloody thing. If the homeowners care enough about their house to get someone to mind it, they probably also care enough to have installed a highly sophisticated burglar alarm system that you'll never be able to disarm properly when you get home pissed at two in the morning. And the security alarm company, the police and the neighbours will all get a bit fed up with the alarm going off every night of the week.*

4. **Boarding** *Just like living in a hotel except there's no room service, no colour TV, no mini-bar, no decent furniture and certainly no friendly or helpful staff.*

5. **Renting** *Apart from having to live with a bunch of humourless housemates, the biggest problem with rental accommodation is working out how to get your deposit back when you've finally been kicked out.* (Hint: draw curtains or blinds in bedroom to disguise broken window panes and rearrange all bedroom furniture to cover any large holes in the walls.)

Lodging with your landlady made uncommonly tense

- Ask her if she is declaring all income from the lodgers to the taxman.
- Bring a boyfriend to your room at night.
- Hang around the house on the weekend.
- Hang around the house on week nights.
- Take a hot bath, daily.
- Come in after ten o'clock at night – drunk.
- Lose your keys and bang loudly on the door after ten o'clock at night – drunk.
- Forget to lock the front door behind you.
- Leave your bedroom window open when you go out.
- Leave the iron on when you go out.
- Leave lights on when you go out.
- Fill the kettle full of water when you're only making a coffee for one.
- Ask if you can turn on the heating.

Getting your flat-mates to move out without having to ask

- Fling all your belongings into the biggest bedroom as soon as you move in.
- Refuse to let your flat-mate store any of her belongings under your king-size bed or inside your walk-in wardrobe.
- Eat everything in the fridge that your flat-mate has marked "PLEASE DO NOT EAT".
- Refuse to stay in your bedroom when you flat-mate is having a dinner party.
- Use the last of the milk every morning.
- Use the last of the hot water every morning.
- Use the last of the toilet roll every evening.
- Refuse to get out of the bath until you've finished reading *War and Peace*.
- Fall asleep half way through it.
- Buy lots of fruit and vegetables and then leave them to rot in the fridge.
- Encourage friends overseas to ring late at night.
- Deny making long-distance calls when the phone bill comes in.
- Forget to pass on phone messages.
- Leave your underwear to dry on radiators throughout the house.
- Convert the dining or living area into your home-office.
- Leave your wet clothes in the washing machine when the cycle has finished.
- Throw out newspapers and magazines before your flat-mate has read them.
- Borrow your flat-mate's clothes, make-up or car without asking.

Upsetting the neighbours without really trying

- Play loud music late at night on weekdays.
- Play loud music during the day on weekends.
- Play anything by Motorhead, Metallica or Mariah Carey.
- Buy a creaking bed.
- Have noisy, graphic sex in the creaking bed.
- Knock on the party wall when your neighbours are having noisy, graphic sex in their equally as creaking bed.
- Start hammering, drilling, vacuuming or tap-dancing after ten o'clock in the evening.
- Learn to play the drums, the bagpipes or the bass guitar.
- Flood your washing machine (only applicable if you live above the ground floor).
- Open and read your neighbours' post.
- Steal their home-delivered magazines, newspapers and catalogues.
- Shove all your junk mail into their letter-box.
- Use their rubbish bin.
- Snitch on them for not having a television licence.
- Ask them if they've got council planning permission for the shed that they're building in their back garden.
- Forget to feed their pets when they're on holiday.
- Forget to water their plants when they're on holiday.
- Ring them when they're on holiday to tell them they've been burgled.
- Steal their Neighbourhood Watch sign rather than buy your own.

Crime Watch
To deter burglars, only buy ugly, expensive things.

I'VE OWNED HANDBAGS BIGGER THAN THIS

Why Owning Your Own Home Isn't Worth It

Buying a house is almost as big a drain on your finances as owning a couple of store cards. Furthermore, unless you've got really rich parents or a really rich partner or a lucrative contract with *Hello!* magazine, you won't be able to afford many bricks for your bucks. Worse still, when you haul out a stray cat from your handbag and start swinging it around your head in order to prove a point to the anxious vendors and the eager estate agent in front of you, you'll end up covered in plaster, mould and dry rot as your four-legged friend bounces off the walls, floors and ceilings.

Selling Point

To disguise subsidence problems when selling your house, lean in the same direction as the walls while you're showing potential buyers around.

Reasons against purchasing a property

You'll start to feel at home in your new house and begin to make some
money from it, only after you have:

- Paid the solicitor.
- Paid the pest control people.
- Changed all the locks on external windows and doors.
- Fixed the boiler.
- Fitted the new wood venetian blinds.
- Fitted the new wood toilet seat.
- Ripped up the carpets.
- Laid down the new polished floorboards.
- Painted the walls.
- Replastered the ceiling.
- Eradicated the damp problem.
- Replaced all the light fittings.
- Rewired the old power points.
- Installed built-in wardrobes.
- Ripped out the old kitchen.
- Installed the new kitchen.
- Installed cable television.
- Repaired broken windows.
- Installed the double-glazing.
- Re-tiled the bathroom.
- Mended the dripping taps.
- Unblocked the drains.
- Bought lots of new furniture.
- Bought lots of new outdoor plants.
- Got the tenants above, below or next door evicted.
- Paid off the interest on the mortgage.
- Paid off the mortgage.

Reasons for selling a property

If you're loathe to invest time, money and emotional outbursts on a property, you're likely to own the sort of place that can only be improved upon by wearing a very dark pair of sunglasses.

Fortunately, this does not pose a major problem when it comes to getting rid of the thing, providing you lack principles, morals and scruples – or have the name of a really good estate agent.

FOR SALE

Small (you can go to the toilet without having to stop stirring a pan of sauce on the oven hot-plate), **charming** (the rats are quite tame), **recently refurbished** (you fitted one of the water pipes with a new washer last year) **and very secure abode** (the owner before you left behind his switchblade), **with lots of light** (you've just bought a new torch) **and lots of potential** (for some other idiot maybe). **Close to public transport** (can get to the station in less than five minutes if the water levels are down), **shops** (there's a shopping centre right above you), **and situated in a quiet residential area** (you can't hear much when you're hundreds of feet under the ground). **Would suit young professional person** (who doesn't have to look at it or live in it for at least 38 hours a week) **or first–time buyer** (who hasn't got any choice but to dwell in a sewer).

KNITTING PATTERNS NOT INCLUDED

Housekeeping Hints For Bone-Idle Bad Girls

If you're too old to take your washing to your mum's place but too young to qualify for Meals on Wheels, then sooner or later you're going to have to learn to cook and clean for yourself.

This isn't as difficult as it sounds, providing you don't mind starving on a regular basis or wearing reversible clothing. It also helps if you're not allergic to dust or bed mites or those strange and foul smells emerging from the rubbish bag you've been meaning to take out of the house for the last three-and-a-half weeks.

Things you should have in your fridge-freezer

Half a tub of moisturizer.

Bottle of eye drops.

Two rotting carrots.

Half a head of limp lettuce.

One onion.

Open tin of cat food (hopefully only if you've got a cat).

Bottle with dregs of cheap white wine.

Empty carton of semi-skimmed milk.

Neolithic tub of low-fat strawberry yoghurt.

Small cube of cheese.

Empty ice cube tray.

Two bottles of vodka.

Things you may find in your cupboard

Tin of plum tomatoes.

Packet of two-minute noodles well past its use-by date.

Can of sardines.

Salt.

Pepper.

Small jar of cocktail cherries.

Packet of toothpicks.

Miscellaneous button.

Mouse droppings.

Three hair grips.

Empty mini-jar of Nescafé.

Things you won't find in your cupboard

Freshly ground coffee beans.

Virgin olive oil.

Dried fruit

Assorted nuts

Jar of artichokes

Jar of pesto

Savoury biscutis

After dinner mints

Packet of stuffing for 20lb turkey

FIVE-MINUTE RECIPE
Primeval Soup

Three rotting carrots
Half a head of limp lettuce
One onion
Packet of two-minute noodles well past its use-by date
Tin of plum tomatoes
Dregs of cheap white wine
Salt
Pepper

1. Open bottle of vodka.
2. Pour generous measure into a glass.
3. Drink it.
4. Take all the ingredients listed above (apart from the salt and pepper) and bung them uncaringly into a stained and cracked pot.
5. Turn pot on to high.
6. Pour another generous measure of vodka into a glass and continue drinking until you notice or hear pot boiling over.
7. Fish out plastic noodle packet and remove softened onion skin.
8. Take quick swig of vodka again for Dutch courage.
9. Season soup to taste, pull a face then toss pot and contents into bin.
10. Disguise disgusting smell by turning music up really loud.
11. To stave off hunger pangs, finish off bottle of vodka.

Other domestic tips for the completely clueless

- Save on grocery bills by collecting sachets of dried soup, noodles and milk drinks found stuck between the pages of various women's magazines.
- If you don't have any books on your shelves, cereal packets make an excellent and cheap alternative.
- Always stock up on kitchen roll in case you run out of toilet roll.
- Rather than having to continually sweep up crumbs from the kitchen floor, pick up a starving pet from the pound.
- Shampoo is an adequate substitute for washing-up liquid.
- Washing-up liquid is an adequate substitute for shampoo.
- Always keep a can of sardines in the cupboard. (You'll never eat them, but at least you know they'll always be there.)
- Save hours of tedious ironing by sending out all your clothes to the dry cleaners.
- Rather than buying tea cosies or oven mitts, put your best lambs' wool sweaters in a hot wash cycle.
- Use last season's clothes as emergency dusters and tea towels.
- Get out of bed at inconvenient hours of the night to tape programmes rather than read the video recorder instruction manual.
- If you have clothes you can't bear to throw away but know will never be worn again, burn them with the iron.
- Marry a man who doesn't eat much.
- Marry a man who is house-proud.

Safety Tip
Smoke alarms make great substitutes for oven timers whenever you're cooking a meal.

WHERE'S YOUR WORK VISA THEN?

Finding Good Help And Treating Them Badly

Just because you're a bad girl, doesn't mean to say you don't have a conscience or a sense of community spirit. Quite the contrary, in fact. You much prefer giving money to people less fortunate than yourself so that you can avoid doing all the annoying little chores around your home. Illegal immigrants, political refugees and students on welfare all benefit from your cash-in-hand hand-outs. Best of all, if they start taking your good nature for granted by refusing to cater, dust or dig to your every whim, you can always threaten to hand them over to the relevant government department.

Things to get your cleaning lady to do:
- Colour co-ordinate your cotton balls.
- Pick off the shreds of the tissue you left in a cardigan pocket when you were doing your washing.
- Put all your compact discs back into their correct cases.

Things to get your nanny to do:
- Take your kids to the dry cleaners to pick up your garments.
- Take your kids to the supermarket to do the weekly shopping.
- Take your kids to the car wash to get your car cleaned.

Things to get your cook to do:

- Order your nightly pizza home deliveries for you.
- Refill ice-cube trays.
- Pull corks from wine bottles.

Things to get your gardener to do:

- Drain artificial ponds and pools and then fill them with gravel.
- Take plants, shrubs, flowers, trees and other compost materials to the rubbish tip.
- Resurface the lawn with patio tiles.

Dirty Thought
To turn on a washing machine, simply take off your clothes.

4.2 BAD GIRLS ON THE MOVE

"If I had to live my life again, I'd make all the same mistakes – only sooner."
Tallulah Bankhead

Life in the fast lane isn't all it's cracked up to be. Jet-setting around isn't always the best way to go. While beaming, blonde TV presenters on crap, low-budget travel shows might urge you to stop living vicariously through beaming, blonde TV presenters on crap, low-budget travel shows, they get paid to get out and about in the real world. And, when they do, they travel first-class and stay in five-star hotels. You, on the other hand, are required to hand over your hard-earned wages just so you can mingle with drunken tourists, unhelpful foreigners and a hatchet-faced air steward who resents being stuck in economy class. The only consolation about travelling away from home is that at least you'll be free of beaming, blonde TV presenters on crap, low-budget travel shows (until, of course, you discover that your motel room's got cable).

As well as ticking off less-than-exotic destinations and bolshy bell-boys, this girls-on-the-go travel guide also explores the theories that: planes invite mid-air collisions with drinks trolleys; public transport incites bus fines and rail rage; taxi-drivers inspire muttered comments about English-As-A-Second-Language evening classes; and pedestrians are just accidents waiting to happen when you're the one driving the car.

Travel Tip
To discover warm and friendly hospitality on your travels, always carry large amounts of cash.

I FORFEITED MY ANNUAL HOLIDAY LEAVE FOR THIS?

Going To Hell and Back On Your Days Off Work

Misgivings about holidays usually start the minute you're on one. What may seem like redeeming features on the home front are not necessarily such desirable traits abroad. Mouthing off at your mother down the phone isn't quite in the same league as squaring up to six gun-toting mercenaries at a Mozambique checkpoint. And while spinning yarns to high street assistants in order to exchange a dress you wore only twice might be a breeze, you're going to need to have a much bigger imagination when Customs and Excise inquire why you've got three dozen bottles of duty-free Dior perfume stashed in your hand luggage.

What to pack in your bag to be on the safe side

Toilet rolls.

Tampons.

Condoms.

Laxatives.

Mosquito net.

Fly repellent.

Cough mixture.

Suntan Lotion (Factor 15).

Chapstick.

Bottled water.

Tinned food.

Clean sheets.

Hot towels.

Sterile needles.

Prescription drugs.

Medical encyclopaedia.

Plasters.

Bandages.

Walking sticks.

Collapsible wheelchair.

Portable x-ray machine.

Stomach pump.

Can of mace.

American dollars.

Essential phrases to learn in languages other than your own

That's the last time I'm flying with [insert any airline here].

Can anyone speak English in this goddamned hell-hole?

Drop dead, pervert.

Taxi! Taxi!...Could you save us both a lot of grief and just take me the longest possible route to my hotel?

What do you mean, there's no booking?

What do you mean, my travel agent's gone bust?

What do you mean, my travel insurance won't cover it?

Yes, I suppose the broom cupboard next to the hotel generator will have to do.

Have these mattresses been sprayed recently?

Where's the ensuite bathroom?

Could you get someone up here now. There's a rat attached to my foot.

Call yourself a doctor? Even I could have sewn my leg back on better than that.

What does a girl have to do to get a drink around here?

Drop dead, pervert.

Waiter, waiter. There's a fly in my soup.

Sorry, my mistake. You're quite right. It's only a cockroach.

If I see another crumbling old ancient monument, I'm going to scream. Arrrrgghh!

What's that in proper money?

Come again?

I thought you lot were supposed to be poor and needy.

Do you take AMEX?

Alright then, take your cheap and nasty imitation African death mask and shove it where the sun doesn't shine.

I thought you lot were supposed to be warm and friendly.

Take me to the embassy at once.

Places to avoid on your travels

Africa Too many dead tourists.

Antarctica Too many environmentalists.

Australia Too many cricket fans.

Canada Too many chips on too many shoulders about being mistaken for Americans.

China Too many cyclists.

Eastern Europe Too many snipers.

Iceland Too many Bjork fans.

India Too many backpackers.

Middle East Too many men.

New Zealand Too many New Zealanders.

North America Too many fat people.

Russia Too many *nouveau riche* people.

South East Asia Too many drug convictions.

South America Too many street kids.

United Kingdom Too many old buildings.

Western Europe Too many different accents.

Baggage Claim

Only ever allow a boyfriend to accompany you on a trip if you've got a lot of heavy luggage that you don't want to carry.

CAN I HAVE MY MONEY BACK, PLEASE?

Ways To Behave Like A Tourist Abroad

- Whinge about being homesick within minutes of arriving.
- Refuse to go on any tours of local museums, galleries, markets, churches and statues.
- If you do go on any of the aforementioned tours, ask out loud how many crumbling old relics you're expected to admire in one day.
- Never bring your boyfriend – why pay good money to do it with him in Tobago when you can get it at home in Chipping Sodbury for nothing?
- If you do bring your boyfriend along for the ride, sulk the minute his attention shifts from you to, say, the Sistine Chapel.
- Go along with everything your boyfriend wants to do, and then hold it against him for the rest of your life.
- Get drunk and dance on bar counters just to prove that the loud and noisy ones at home are also the biggest embarrassments abroad.
- Relive your youth at an all-night beach rave and pretend not to notice the 20-year age gap.
- Remain oblivious to scowls and glares from young children on the beach who resent a grown woman borrowing their frisbees, beach balls, and buckets and spades.
- Refuse to learn the native tongue so you don't actually have to talk to the natives.
- Refuse to participate in any adventure holiday activity that makes you bleed, sweat, cry or look unattractive in general.
- Never stay anywhere that doesn't have room service and valet parking.
- Refuse to do anything that involves chasing your own food.
- Refuse to carry a backpack.

- Refuse to listen to the tour guide because you don't want to be lectured at by an out-of-work actor.
- Wander off from your coach tour party when everyone is dying to get back to the hotel.

The Seven Major Disappointments of the World

1. **The Louvre, Paris** *Full of old junk.*

2. **Harrods, London** *Full of expensive junk.*

3. **Disneyland, Los Angeles** *Too many queues for the rides.*

4. **World Trade Centre, New York** *Too many queues for the lifts.*

5. **Ayers Rock (Uluhru), Central Australia** *Looks just like a rock.*

6. **The Great Wall of China** *Looks just like a wall.*

7. **Lenin's Tomb, Moscow** *Corpse looks like it's just escaped from Madame Tussaud's.*

Travel Tip

To add a little spontaneity to an otherwise boring trip abroad, always make sure you lose your passport, your travellers' cheques and your luggage – preferably all at once.

NOT WHERE I COME FROM, YOU DON'T

Why Sex Overseas Is Over-Rated

Right. You've packed your suitcase and managed to wedge in all your black, cherry-flavoured, edible knickers plus the bulk-box of donkey-sized condoms. Now you're on a plane tightly sandwiched between a heavy-breathing Japanese businessman who still thinks he's in the Tokyo subway and an Albanian nun who keeps casting you dirty looks. That's when the cold dreads hit you. Damn. You've forgotten your *Loathesome Planetary Guide to Holiday Bonks*. Fret not, my dearies, help is at hand. Just read the following itinerary and you'll find out everything you didn't want to know about sex overseas.

First stop is **New York**, city of many single females and one smug single male. The fact that he's shagged all the desperate single females doesn't bother you – indeed, it adds a certain *frisson* to polite conversation when you and he bump into them all on the streets. The fact that he's forgetful during introductions doesn't deter you either. After all, The Big Apple's a huge place and he can't be expected to remember the names of all its female inhabitants – particularly yours. No, it's the frequent disappearing acts that really get to you – particularly when you're the one left to deal with the hysterical Jasmines, Yasmeens and Phoebes who knock on his door late at night. When you question the validity of conducting an affair with someone who isn't around to support you when you're faced with a knife-wielding woman, he says you should feel honoured that he's letting you fight for him. Incapable of arguing with such logic, you let Jasmine, Yasmeen or Phoebe into the apartment and point pointedly under the bed.

Next you coast down to **Miami** and enter one of those awful 18-35 offshore resorts where social outcasts from Wales go to make friends.

He isn't usually allowed to travel so far from home but his parents sold three sheep and a leek field in order to send him as far away from them as possible. During Happy Hour at the bar, when you're absolutely rat-faced on cocktails and would shag anything that moved, he sidles up because a) he's never one to miss a rare opportunity, and b) he knows he won't have to buy you a drink since you'll throw up if you have one more Orgasm (which is one less than you'll ever have with him). Fed up with trying to understand what he's saying, you resolve to go white-water rafting down the Amazon because you've heard the insects there are better looking.

Of course, a Californian bimbo can't think to save his life which is why you'll end up saving it for him when you meet him down a dark alley in **Rio**, where swarthy natives are threatening to smash his pretty face in because he's been flexing his muscles at their girlfriends. As your reward for protecting his boyish good looks, he presents you with an itsy-bitsy, teeny-weeny yellow polka-dot bikini. Of course, having just trekked through the rainforests you haven't had time to have a decent shave. At the sight of all that excess body hair, and despite your wonderful, warm personality, he'll flee into the night again.

Naturally, you leap on to the first **Caribbean** cruise liner you come across in search of a razor blade or at least a bloke with a bit of depth. Unfortunately, the only single man aboard, (apart from the widowers in the wheelchairs) is a Belgian who insists upon mixing business with pleasure and plaid with polyester. Charming all the old ladies rigid with his life insurance sales pitches might be his ideas of a good time but even the tanned, toothsome, and gay recreation officer would prefer to jump overboard and compare dental records with the sharks.

You follow suit and end up washed up in **Nairobi**. Here, an attractively aloof man with bad breath and body odour orders you to have sex on safari with him. Of course, only a Frenchman would be contemptuous enough to get out of the four-wheel drive, fold his arms and with a curl of his lip say, "Where are all zee so-called wild animals, then?" Before you have time to scream, "Behind you, you imbecile!" a large and lethal-looking beast is mauling and pawing him (at last giving him a taste of his own medicine). You spend valuable holiday time nursing him back to health in a corrugated-iron toilet disguised as a hospital, while he makes passes at all the female patients and unwittingly offends the doctor by declaring the Ebola virus a third world conspiracy to attract more tourist dollars.

So you beat it to **Bangkok,** home to hagglers, hustlers and the Australian bloke. He's easy to spot, particularly in ping-pong parlours. He's the bonehead trying to catch the balls in his mouth while two dozen other low-brows egg him on. The latter are his antipodean mates because he always prefers to travel in a pack. These same jokers are the ones who think it's clever and funny to bounce his hostel bed up and down while he's grunting on top of you. Romance turns sour when you start acting "like a typical bloody Sheila" after he declares the native girls more feminine, agreeable and broad-minded – though just wait until one of them is mailed back to him in Oz and has to put up with the great lug forever.

Sick of having to step over his knuckles every time you need to go to the bathroom, you hot-foot it to **Nepal** for some spiritual relief. Here you chance upon the kind of weirdly charismatic man who gives British backpackers a bad name. This one is trying to find himself or, failing that, at least another meal ticket. The long-haired hippies following him are not his acolytes, no matter how many times he tries to tell you otherwise. They're all his pissed-off girlfriends from back home in England who refuse to let him get away with shagging his way around the world in the name of racial harmony. You'd love to stay and seduce him silly except his pompous monologue about injustices done to the dirty and disfigured puts you off at the pivotal moment. You also think it's rich of him to be preaching about wealth distribution when his Visa card is in credit yet he's still sponging off you.

So it's on to **Saudi Arabia**. Not out of choice, but because the bunch of tea-towelled lunatics waving machine guns in a maniacal manner in the cockpit make it a mandatory stopover. Once the crack Israeli commando squad has got you safely off the plane, you're herded into the airport where a clean-shaven, clean-cut, well-spoken, Old Etonian politely offers to buy you an orange juice. Yes, you have just been propositioned by an Arabian arms dealer. No drinking, no drugs, no sex with the lights on. And definitely not unless you wear your veil (which would probably be a good thing as then he wouldn't see you grinding your teeth and rolling your eyes during his extremely protracted and massively unsuccessful attempt to locate your G-spot). After he's had a nice, cleansing shower – even though you didn't actually do anything – he asks you to join his harem. Then he hands you a wad of cash and tells you to meet him and his other wives outside a bank in Switzerland, another place full of boring, old-fashioned fuddy-duddies like him who throw themselves off chalet rooftops because they've got nothing better to do on the weekend.

Predictably, you bypass the land of hillocks, pillocks and fondue sets and cycle to **Amsterdam** for some good old-fashioned raunch and reefer instead. The shifty-eyed, long-nosed but good-looking-in-a-Celtic-sort-of-way guy in the raincoat at the café is not a pimp or a pervert – though he does admire and respect women, particularly his mother. Without a word of a lie, he tells you he's living here because its sense of history appeals to his romantic Irish soul. You point out that there are crumbly old buildings everywhere in Europe, not all of them featuring naked women writhing around in windows. Nevertheless, in his squalid bedsit you shag him senseless. This takes approximately one-and-a-half seconds excluding the time it takes to put on and then take off his condom. Afterward you ask him for a commitment and he comes down with a chronic attack of the Catholic guilts and says he can't give you one because a) you're not his mother and b) you're not a virgin.

Agreeing with him whole-heartedly, you mooch on down to **Munich** and fall over a lager lout. He's on one of those let's-drink-ourselves-sick-through-Europe-instead-of-at-home-in-Scotland tours and you find him slouched under a trestle table in a beer tent. He gets pissed off when you challenge him to a skolling contest and win. However, because he's willing to forgive you (because you bought the drinks), you make the mistake of allowing him to kiss you. This drunken ordeal is enough to make you wish Scotsmen came with energy performance ratings stars like fridges do.

So now it's off to **Rome** where you get bowled by a tall, dark, brooding stranger careering his car down the wrong side of the street. If the fact that he tells you he's Sicilian isn't a give-away, the tinted car windows and gravelly voice should be a huge clue. And let's be honest here: the violin case should have set alarm bells ringing, especially since you now know he's tone deaf because you heard him warbling the theme tune from *The Godfather* on the way down south to meet his family. Typical – only you could start off as a carefree holiday-maker and end up as a Mafia moll. Of course, he's married. But then again most Italians are. Life in his household is perfect for the five minutes before you realize that rampant sex is very well and good, and conducive to weight loss, but all that talk about honour, trust and loyalty is nothing short of emotional abuse. When he's in the bathroom calling his wife on the intercom, you make your dash for freedom, now being svelte enough to slip through the bars on the window.

Next it's straight down to the **Greek Isles** to flop at the feet of the handsome Lothario who owns a small wine bar and an even smaller you-know-what. The one mere mortal who makes Narcissus look modest, is baking in the sun and staring at his reflection in your Ray Bans. He's surrounded by a bevy of breast-enhanced beauties peeling him olives in a futile attempt to get his attention. If you didn't know better you'd think he was God. Accept, of course, Our Father Who Art In Heaven isn't half as attractive. Or intelligent. Or witty. Inevitably, you do all the wrong things: you send him on menial errands, you forget to tell him how fantastic he looks as he prowls out of the sea, you laugh at him rather than with him. He in turn, orders you off his (sic) island.

By the time you get home you're completely fagged and thanking your lucky stars you'll never hear from any of those losers again. Three days later you find out that you've got the clap from the Frenchman, you get a death threat masquerading as a postcard from the Italian and the M16 machine gun you ordered from the Arab. The Greek sends you his autograph, the British backpacker phones reverse-charges to ask you for money, and the Australian writes you a haiku poem since he can't string more than five words together. Next it's the Californian emoting on a Post-It note, followed by a begging letter from the Welshman who wants you to be his pen-friend. The Belgian priority-posts some super-annuation forms for you to fill in, the Scotsman mails you a souvenir beer mat by sea mail, and the Yank from New York does sweet sod all. And last, but very least, there's a knock at your door. It's that silver-tongued Irishman from old Amsterdam who says he can't live without you and wants to be the father of your children after all. Don't believe him for a second. Young gift-of-the-gab is obviously on the run from Interpol for being caught in a hypocritical position with an underage Protestant prostitute and a set of rosary beads.

Why Don't You?
Do what most men do and always wear dark sunglasses so you can perve at any sexy, young locals without getting told off by your partner.

GETTING FROM A TO B WITH A BUNCH OF C's

A Travel Guide For The Disenchanted

Whoever said that getting there is half the fun was obviously an ironic amputee. Travel of any description is a necessary evil and even then there's a lot to be said for staying in bed all day.

Planes are basically just large buckets of rusty bolts. Cars are really only high-maintenance shopping trolleys. Taxis are simply God's way of punishing you for being too lazy to walk. And public transport is a ticket inspector's idea of cheap thrills when he catches you trying to dodge your fare.

Things To Do If You Hate Walking

- Crawl.
- Chop your legs off.
- Get a piggy-back.
- Hire a sedan chair.
- Buy a pony.
- Buy a pony and trap.
- Pretend you don't own any sensible, flat-heeled shoes.
- Do all your grocery shopping via the internet.
- Do all your grocery shopping via mail order.

Things to do if you hate flying

- Hit passengers on the head with your hand luggage as you move down the aisle to your seat.
- Hit passengers on the head with your hand luggage as you try to put it in the overhead lockers.
- Snore loudly while cabin crew members are acting out the safety demonstration.
- Sit in the crash position for the entire flight.
- Press the "Steward Service" button every couple of minutes and request a drink.
- Put your seat back when the person behind you is attempting to eat from the pull-down meal tray.
- Eat your own meal with both your elbows out.
- Ask the passenger next to you if he wants his dessert.
- Attempt to climb over dozing passengers in the middle and aisle seats in order to get to the toilet.
- When the main aisle lights go out in the evening, put your overhead light on and start to read.
- Listen to the comedy radio channel through your headset and constantly laugh loudly.
- Confuse immigration officials when their eyes go from your face to the one pictured in your passport by wearing sunglasses, a hat, a scarf, a wig and a false moustache.
- Get custom officials' hopes up by looking furtive, sweating a lot and walking in a very peculiar fashion.

Things to do if you hate taxi-drivers

- Slam the cab door really hard when you get in.
- Ask him if he speaks English.
- Tell him you can't understand him either.
- Ask him to take you somewhere.
- Tell him you don't know where it is either.
- Toss him your map and tell him to find it.
- Take the map back, locate the address and hand the map back to him with your finger marking the exact spot.
- Ask him if it's okay to smoke.
- Tell him that if he can't stand the smell of smoke then you can't stand the smell of the pine tree deodorizer hanging from his dashboard and can he throw it out of the window, please?
- Start reading the small print on your shopping bags so he can't start any further conversations.
- Start fretting when he's still driving around three hours later.
- Start fretting even more when he totally refuses to ask passers-by for directions.
- Wind down the window and lean out so that you can ask passers-by for directions.
- Pay him the fare with a five pound note.
- Tell him you don't have any change either.
- Ask him for a written receipt.
- Tell him you don't have a pen either.
- Ask him for your map back.
- Slam the cab door really hard when you get out.

Things to do while you're waiting for a bus

- Look at your watch.
- Realize that the hands on the face are going around too quickly.
- Take the watch to bits.
- Put it back together again.
- Discover there are two cogs left over, so take watch to bits again.
- Put it back together again.
- Adjust your watch to the correct time using the bus timetable on the bus shelter as a guide.
- Then start reading the entire bus timetable.
- Read it again, but this time out loud.
- Read it again out loud, but this time backwards and in Chinese.
- Write a screenplay based on the time you've spent reading the bus timetable out loud backwards and in Chinese.
- Place numerous calls on your mobile and eventually sell the screenplay to Hollywood.
- While the screenplay's still in development, ask a nearby road worker what the time is.
- When he scratches his head and whistles at you, ask if you can borrow his tools while he goes on his tea-break.
- Using a pnuematic drill, a cement mixer and a spade, build an entire city from scratch.
- Get annoyed when dozing road worker wakes up and points out that you've forgotten to allow for a decent bus service.
- Decide to walk to the shops instead.

Things to do while you're waiting for a train to be towed back to the station

- Ask the nearby loud-mouthed idiot, who's been showing off on his mobile for most of the journey, if you can borrow it for a few moments.

- A few seconds later, ring whoever's meant to be picking you up from the station to say you're going to be a few minutes late.

- A few hours later, ring your boss and ask if you can take a couple of days out of your holiday leave.

- A few weeks later, ring your boss back and ask if you can take a couple of months' long-service leave.

- A few years later, ring your lawyer and dictate to him your last will and testament.

- A few decades later, ring the train company's customer service line to complain about the sandwiches in the buffet bar.

- A century later, ring the train company's customer care line to complain about the fact that their customer service line has kept you on hold.

Things to do to keep yourself amused while driving your own car

- Swerve, brake or crash suddenly in order to avoid cyclists.
- Blow your horn at people having picnics on pedestrian crossings.
- Flash your lights at on-coming police cars to let them know there are other cars on the road.
- Wind your window up at traffic lights as soon as you see someone walking towards you rattling a charity tin or brandishing a windscreen mop.
- Wind your window right down while you're playing speed garage really loudly.
- Do a three-point turn – badly – while an ambulance is trying to get past.
- Stop in the middle of a busy intersection during peak hour, put your bonnet up and pretend that your car's broken down.

Fare Comment

If you plan on ram-raiding a shop or robbing a bank, rather than add wear and tear to your own car, why not hail a cab?

4.3 THIS ISN'T THE BRADY BUNCH

"I know I was cruel to other children because I remember stuffing their nostrils with putty, and beating a little boy with stinging nettles."
Vita Sackville-West

Sometimes, just sometimes, you might wish you could break free of pointless traditions. You might wish you could stop arguing with your parents and fighting with your siblings and back-stabbing your friends and cleaning up after pets and visiting senile old great-aunts in the country who always try to force-feed you great wedges of fruitcake. But then, where's the fun in a world without feuds, frictions or Freudian slips? How can you say that your life has true meaning if you can't rub friends and family up the wrong way? And where else are you going to get your yearly allowance of fibre?

Covering familiar unfriendly territories, this incisive portrayal of close relationships will help you to bring out the worst in all of them. Whether it's wedging open the generation gap with an over-sized spanner, clubbing sibling rivals with a giant Lego block, or moving away as far as possible from distant relatives, the foregone conclusion is that everyone around you comes from a parallel dimension; the main aim is to show you how to keep them there.

Parental Guidance

Regular phone calls, frequent visits and suitably expressed gratitude for unasked-for lectures about your love life and dress sense will always guarantee you bigger, better birthday presents from your parents.

WHAT'S WRONG WITH MY TATTOO?

How To Disappoint Your Mum And Your Dad

Parents. Who'd have them? They'll nag you about your nose ring.
They'll complain about your spendthrift ways. They'll tut-tut about
your bad-boy boyfriend and they'll look silently pained when you tell
them it's all their fault you're such a lost cause.

But, no matter how many sick dreams you have about being
secretly adopted or tragically orphaned, it would serve you well to
realize that blood really is thicker than water (even though it's a
bugger to get out of the carpet). Indeed, you could start acting like a
mature, sensible adult and avert full-scale war with your parents by
apologizing first, even if and when it is not your fault. Or by bypassing
their place and getting a boyfriend to fix your car, lend you money and
do your washing and ironing.

Then again, if you refuse to let mum and dad off the hook so
easily, you could just start to dwell on the past. What you find won't
surprise you *or* your parents: you felt misunderstood as a teenager,
abused as a child and downright neglected as a baby. No wonder
you're such a screw-up now.

Things never to forgive or forget your parents for

- Dressing you in blue as a baby because they were expecting a boy.
- Dressing you in yellow because they couldn't be bothered finding out what sex you were before you were born.
- Dressing you in pink as a baby despite the fact that it clashed with your complexion.
- Embarrassing you in public by breastfeeding you.
- Torturing you in private by singing nursery rhymes off-key.
- Making you wear old-fashioned cloth nappies instead of trendier disposable ones.
- Telling you off when you were naughty.
- Putting back all the sweets you put into the supermarket trolley.
- Getting shampoo in your eyes when they were washing your hair in the bath.
- Making you brush your teeth before you went to bed.
- Forgetting to inform the tooth fairy that you'd lost a fang.
- Making you kiss really old relatives.
- Buying you books for your birthday instead of a Barbie.
- Buying you a Barbie for Christmas instead of a bike.
- Making you go to school.
- Making you take your make-up off before you went to school.
- Making you egg sandwiches to take to school for lunch.
- Encouraging you to learn the violin.
- Encouraging you to stick up for yourself in the playground.
- Telling you off for coming home with a black eye and a torn pinafore dress.
- Telling you off for getting a D for Science even though you got a D+ for English.
- Being unable to help you with your Maths homework once you've gone past basic algebra.

- Asking you to help with the washing up.
- Making you tidy your room.
- Checking to see that you've tidied it.
- Embarrassing you by telling you the facts of life.
- Embarrassing you by being the only parents who've not got divorced.
- Embarrassing you by holding hands in public.
- Embarrassing you by running off with a neighbour.
- Embarrassing you by saying hello to your friends.
- Reading your diary.
- Confronting you with its contents.
- Not believing you when you say you made it all up.
- Waiting up for you when you come home late from a date.
- Embarrassing you by asking if you want to go on the pill.
- Getting upset when you say you're already on it.
- Showing your new boyfriend pictures of you as a baby.

Things your parents will say just to annoy you

"You'll never learn, will you?"

"Ask your father."

"Can't you do anything right?"

"Ask your mother."

"I wish you were more like your brother."

"You're just like your father."

"Just wait until he gets home."

"I assume you're coming home for Christmas."

"Don't mind me, I'm just your mother."

"After all I've done for you..."

"You're not going out in that?"

"Have you met anyone special yet?"

"He's such a nice, young man."

"Oh well, it's your funeral."

"I'm not going to say I told you so."

"I told you so."

"What's that you're wearing?"

"Can't you do something with your hair?"

"You've put on weight."

"Why aren't you married yet?"

"I was hoping for some grandkids."

"Why haven't you called?"

...gs you can say just to annoy ...ur parents

"...ve been kicked out of school."

"Do you like my tattoo?"

"I've dropped out of college."

"Can I borrow the car?"

"I've just lost my job again."

"Can I borrow some money?"

"I'm dating a convicted drug dealer."

"Well, at least he's not stuck-up."

"He's only ten years younger than me."

"It's the fashion."

"It was only for selling heroin, for God's sake."

"I'm not coming home for Christmas."

"Can I move back in for a while?"

"I like being single."

"I don't want to go out and have fun."

"I'm moving out."

"I'm dating an unemployed actor."

"He's only 15 years older than me."

"He's got three kids."

"He hasn't got round to getting a divorce."

"I don't want to get married."

"I like living in sin."

"I don't care what the neighbours will say."

"I don't want kids of my own."

"I'm pregnant."

"You did sleep with Dad before you were married."

"You were pregnant with me before you were married."

"Well, I didn't ask to be born."

Things to do when you start to sound like your Mum

- Kill yourself.

Things to do when you start to sound like your Dad

- Cut back on the steroids.

Courting Technique

If your parents are exceptionally strait-laced and catch you in a compromising embrace with a male outside the front door late at night, just pretend that you're being mugged.

IT'S NOT MY FAULT I'M AN ONLY CHILD

Making Bad Behaviour Your Birthright

Use this ranking-by-birth guide, posing as helpful regression therapy, to relive previous slights by your parents, resurrect prior grudges towards your siblings and re-instate your right to be as childish as you want to be when you next visit the family home.

Bad behaviour to blame on Eldest Child Syndrome

- Regular nervous breakdowns caused by pushy, under-achieving parents with high aspirations.
- Refusal to babysit children (particularly nieces and nephews) as a result of having to look after younger siblings in the past.
- Leather and rubber fetish attributable to stern discipline meted out during your youth.

Bad behaviour to blame on Middle Child Syndrome

- Extraordinarily loud voice because you were always ignored when you were a child.
- Refusal to actively seek work owing to living under the shadow of your high-achieving elder sibling.
- Abnormal fear of venturing near supermarkets because you were often left behind in them.

Bad behaviour to blame on Youngest Child Syndrome

- Excessive drinking and drug abuse caused by parental neglect.
- Lack of gratitude for presents as a result of being ridiculously spoilt as a child.
- Acquisition of an eating disorder thanks to the fact that you always had to fight for your food.

Bad behaviour to blame on Only Child Syndrome

- Homicidal tendencies towards parents and relatives caused by the lack of social interaction while growing up.
- A compulsive shopping habit thanks to your parents overcompensating for your lonely childhood.
- Refusal to divide up your Lottery winnings because you were never taught how to share.

Bad behaviour to blame on Twin Syndrome

- Constant scowl caused by the fact that you learnt at a very young age that people could only spot the difference between you and your identical sibling once they'd worked out you were the slightly less attractive one.
- Tattoos, nose rings and green mohican directly attributable to an ever-present fear of losing your identity.
- Strong feelings of paranoia thanks to the fact that everyone used to stare at you and your twin whenever you were in the stroller together.

CAN'T STAY FOR LONG

How To Upset Family Gatherings

Family gatherings can be a source of much shared joy, particularly if you're not invited. A bad girl's highly strung constitution is unsuited to the madness and mayhem that masquerades as a relaxing family get-together. So, after you've stirred up as much trouble as possible between all those stray uncles, maiden aunts, garrulous grandmas and unkissable cousins, make a swift exit and leave them to their own devices.

Births
- Deliberately shoot the delivery scene without putting any film in the video camera.
- Cast the father-to-be filthy looks for putting your friend through so much agony.
- Ask the mother-to-be if you can have some of her drugs.
- Ask the nurse if it's true that most hospital staff are drug addicts.

Christenings
- Refuse to be a godmother on account that you don't want to be bled dry for the next 18 years.
- Abuse the priest for splashing water on your new, dry-clean-only silk shirt.
- Bitch to the mother about her child-rearing skills.
- Refuse to hold the baby because you've got your best suit on.

Birthdays

- Accidentally leave price tags on expensive gifts.
- Start sulking because you're not the centre of attention.
- Refuse to hand over your lighter when it comes to lighting the birthday candles.
- Sing *Happy Birthday* loudly and out of tune.

Weddings

- Always wear black, even if you are a bridesmaid.
- Turn up later than the bride to the church.
- Leave your mobile phone on during the ceremony.
- Complain loudly about the food at the reception.

Golden Anniversaries

- Buy the loving, though highly superstitious, couple a set of gold-plated knives.
- Talk to the loving couple at length about your current and highly traumatic divorce.
- Start an argument between the loving couple.
- Ask the loving couple about their sex life.

Funerals

- Forget the name of the deceased.
- Ask weeping guests if anything is the matter.
- Tell the driver of the hearse to hurry up.
- Ask if you can take one of the floral arrangements home.

Christmas

- Upset your older relatives by buying motorbikes for their kids.
- Refuse to wear a stupid, crappy paper hat from a stupid, crappy Christmas cracker.
- Pretend that you're on a wheat-free, fat-free, sugar-free, vegetarian diet.
- Tell children under five that there really is no such thing as Father Christmas.

Old Chestnuts

To compensate for not talking to them, tell your grandparents you didn't recognize them as they've aged quite a lot since you saw them last; to compensate for not visiting them, tell them you thought they were dead.

The Happy Families Drinking Game

To survive any large social event involving family members and relatives, you need to get as paralytic as possible, as soon as possible. So down a stiff double every time any one of the following happens:

- Someone falls out with someone else on the day.
- Someone is not speaking to someone else on the day.
- Someone refuses to show up because of a long-standing feud.
- Someone shows up pregnant.
- Someone shows up engaged.
- Someone shows up someone else.
- You meet a cousin you never knew you had.
- You meet a cousin you wish you never had.
- A grandmother keeps getting your name wrong.
- A grandfather keeps muttering about the war.
- A godchild keeps asking you for money.
- A baby cries.
- A mother starts changing a nappy.
- A mother starts breast-feeding in front of you.
- Two children start fighting.
- One gets a nose bleed.
- A mother screams at them to behave.
- A relative's pet bites you.
- Someone asks you if you're married yet.
- Someone asks if you're gay.
- Someone drops a glass.
- Someone eats like a pig.
- Someone decides to get the accordion out.
- Your mother looks like she's about to have a nervous breakdown.
- Your father looks like he'd prefer to be somewhere else.
- Your father-in-law casts you a lecherous glance.

- Your mother-in-law casts you a disapproving look.
- Your brother-in-law tells an off-colour joke.
- Your sister-in-law scowls at you for encouraging him.
- An uncle gets so drunk he falls off his chair.
- An aunt gets so drunk she starts taking off her clothes.
- One of the men in the group falls asleep.
- One of the women in the group bursts into a flood of tears and runs out of the room.
- Your sister bitches to you about your brother.
- Your brother bitches to you about your sister.
- You catch your brother or your sister bitching about you behind your back.
- One of your nephews throws up.
- One of your nieces plays with your make-up bag and wrecks your best lipstick.
- You don't notice because you're completely paralytic at the time.

Festive Tip

Always send out your Christmas cards early to ensure you get plenty back.

DO YOU WANT MY HONEST OPINION?

How To Alienate Your Girlfriends

A bad girl is seldom unpopular. Other girls* flock to her side and clamour for her company because she's invariably interesting, she's witty and she's smart. That's not to say the feeling is mutual. A bad girl tires of being a crowd-pleaser very quickly.

So if you're actively trying to cull all the slavish pups and adoring fans posing as pals, read on – after this, you'll be lucky to count your girlfriends on one finger let alone on a whole hand.

*I am assuming that bad girls only have friends of the female persuasion. Males that surround her are either lovers (which discounts the "friend" bit), potential lovers (which means they're only pretending to be friends in the hope of getting a shag) or gay (which is the same as having a friend of the female persuasion).

1. **Don't encourage friends in need** *Stop girlfriends whining about their appalling boyfriends, once and for all. A humanitarian, charitable approach is a no-no. Instead, breed resentment by being a little less sensitive to a friend's problems during trying times. For instance, if she's broken up with a man, it's a little late in the day to tell her you always knew he was a good-for-nothing scumbag and who'd want to shag him anyway? Rather than nursing her hangovers, wiping her teary eyes, and bailing her out of custody for slashing the tyres of his cars, why not just stop introducing her to your ex-boyfriends in the first place?*

2. Avoid being over-critical *A girlfriend's terrible choices in men, clothes and music is par for the course. Revel in and, indeed, encourage the errors of her ways – after all, it'll make you appear all that more perfect.*

3. Know thine enemy *While competition among girlfriends is perfectly natural, fighting over a man is undignified, especially if it's done in a public place during happy hour and particularly if that man is her boyfriend. Wait until she's passed out in a drunken stupour under the table before you make your move on him.*

4. A true friend will never forgive you *If you're trying to lose a girlfriend, honesty is always the best policy. Be the bearer of bad news – tell her you saw the dress she bought at full-price marked down by 50 per cent. Encourage her to shoot the messenger – tell her what a mutual friend of you both really thinks of her. And try not to make promises you cannot keep just because you're frightened of offending her. Always have the courage to say "No", even if she's attached to a dialysis machine and asks to borrow one of your kidneys.*

5. Find out who your real friends are *Any girl can be popular if she's won the lottery, got a job behind a bar and knows a man with lots of single male mates. Put so-called girlfriends to the test by telling them that you're jobless, homeless, penniless, lovelorn, and feeling suicidal. Then immediately discard those who choose to stick by you. They obviously just want to gloat.*

Friendly Advice
To get rid of unwanted friends why not lend them some money?

Nice things to say to girlfriends when you don't really mean it

"Yes, I definitely think he likes you."

"I'm sure he'll call."

"It doesn't matter who calls who first."

"It looks far better on you than it does on me."

"He's lovely."

"You make a great couple."

"You lucky thing."

"I'm so jealous."

"I wish I was you."

"Yes, I'd love to come over for dinner."

"It's delicious."

"I can't believe you cooked it yourself."

"Thanks for a lovely evening."

"You weren't *that* drunk."

"Of course you didn't make a fool of yourself."

"I can't believe that he would cheat on you."

"He wasn't good enough for you anyway."

"If it makes you feel better, then ring him."

"If it makes you feel better, go round and see him."

"Of course you can stay for the night."

"You don't have to leave yet."

"I don't mind listening."

"You're not boring me."

"It's perfectly understandable."

"I'd have done the same thing myself."

"Yes, you're much prettier than she is – sorry, was."

"Of course, I won't tell anyone."

"Well, the police didn't hear it from me."

HERE, KITTY, KITTY

How To Frighten The Animals

They smell. They fart. They belch. They snore. They grunt. They slobber. They lose their hair. And that's just the men in your life. The last thing you need is something feathered, furred, finned, fanged or flea-bitten to nursemaid as well. Remember, while a pet is for life, a boyfriend never is.

However, if you are a glutton for punishment or if some idiot friend presents you with a cardboard box punctured with air-holes at Christmas, then you're just going to have to make the best of a pretty grim situation.

Why you should buy a pet You've got no other real friends.

What you should buy Almost anything, so long as it's hideously ugly and thus no competition.

Where to buy it from Preferably from a taxidermist. If this should prove impossible, try pounds, paddocks, roadsides and other people's back gardens.

What to name it Oy, Scat, Beg, Down, Bugger-Off or Just-Wait-Till-I-Get-My-Hands-On-You.

How to toilet train it Hah, hah, hah, hah, hah, hah, hah.

When to have it put down When you realize it can't be toilet trained.

What not to buy:

Budgie Teaching it to abuse visitors gets a bit boring after a while.

Cat Own one of these and people will think you're on the shelf.

Dog Tends to hog all the bedclothes.

Duck Too tempting to eat it rather than feed it.

Hamster Lacks a certain *je ne sais quoi*.

Rabbit Can cause feelings of envy if it has a better sex life than you.

Tortoise Its shell may clash with your decor.

What to buy:

Goat Eats everything in its path which means you never have to pick dirty underwear off the floor.

Goldfish Usually dies within a week.

Guinea Pig Excellent for testing your drugs on.

Horse Especially anarchic if you live in a tower block.

Pot-bellied Pig Makes you feel positively svelte in comparison.

Rat You can name it after your ex.

Snake An ideal draught excluder or car alarm.

Pet Care Tip

To avoid having to look after other people's pets, try to make sure you're out of town during the holiday season.

4.4 SEARCHING FOR THE EXIT SIGNS

"When choosing between two evils, I always like to take the one I've never tried before."
Mae West

Bad girls go out – a lot. They go to pubs and clubs and restaurants. They get invited to parties and reunions and days at the races. They get free tickets to the theatre and the opera and the ballet. They get thrown out of cinemas and galleries and restaurants. So it's not surprising they often seem cynical and frequently feel jaded. Sure, if you're wicked, there's amusement to be had in all sorts of social engagements. But bitter experience will have taught you that it can never be found anywhere in a roomful of people.

WHO INVITED YOU LOT?

The Very Shocking Diary Of A Sociopathic Socialite

THURSDAY
6pm: The Local Pub
Go to a pub in a lower socio-demographic area to mingle with the masses – just for a laugh. Ignore lingering looks of mute admiration from polyestered patrons as I make extremely grand entrance dressed head-to-toe in natural fibres.

Shun pool table, giant television screen and pinball machines and head straight for the bar. Forced to order house white because surly bartender says he doesn't stock Bolly. Wine is utterly foul so immediately start checking for cat's hairs at the bottom of my glass. Then pretend to be deeply absorbed in reading a beer mat because I didn't bring a proper book and I don't want to be harassed by the locals.

Of course, four house whites and seven tabby hairs later, am still beating off proles with my Prada bag. One particularly down-at-heel type even has the temerity to ask if I want to go out for a kebab – no doubt thinking I'd be so ill afterwards I wouldn't put up much of a struggle when he made off with my purse. Use complex sentence structures like "Piss off, peasant" to get rid of him. Then bid a speedy *adieu* to my new best friends as soon as they start an impromptu dart-throwing competition.

7pm: An Art Gallery

Am now standing, complimentary bottle of Bolly and tray of canapés in hand, in front of an abstract oil-on-canvas, trying to work out whether it will go with the new rug I've bought for my living room. Eventually decide that it won't, since my rug is green and the painting is crap. Unfortunately, my voice tends to carry in large rooms crammed full of honking, barking, arts *aficionados* so the artist himself hears my generous appraisal. Clearly piqued that I don't like having to suffer for his art, he flounces over and asks me to leave.

I only agree if he can tell me how much profit he makes on a £50,000 picture after taking into account taxes and the cost of one tube of Burnt Sienna. At this stage, the over-possessive gallery owner decides to enter the fray and leap to her protégé's defence. Manage to wrestle her off my back without once spilling my champagne but sadly don't get a chance to throw it at the artwork in question.

Leave gallery empty-handed, except for another bottle of Bolly I swiped from a passing waiter on my way out.

8pm: A Restaurant

Sit in up-market brasserie for half an hour trying to catch a waiter's eye. Finally only manage to get an ashtray when I start stubbing my Marlboro Light out on to the brand new parquet floor. Waiter asks if there is anything wrong with my polenta-radiccio-prosicutto-frittata which is cooling rapidly in front of me. Cast him a look that would be best served in a glass with neat scotch and tell him that I refuse to eat food that ends with a vowel.

He whisks the offending dish away and sweeps off to the kitchen with me hot on his heels. Proceed to give celebrity chef a stern ticking off about his culinary fetishes and then hurl pots and pans back at him in self-defence. Waiter intervenes and asks if I'd like to see the bill but I tell him no because the last time I met a policeman he tried to charge me with aggravated assault.

9.30pm: A Rock Concert

Hate live gigs with a vengeance because bands never sound as good as their records, and audiences who do Mexican waves should be lined up and shot. Only go to this one because I'm positive that the decadent and debauched lead singer is about to be the father of my yet-to-be-conceived, thoroughly lucrative, *News of The World* love-child and I feel I should warn him so he can make sure he's wearing a condom. Get through the three badly-played live sets by listening to the band's album on my personal CD player and as soon as the show's finished, race back-stage to meet up with my caterwauling cash cow.

Elbow all the horrid little groupies out of the way with my french-polished nails and tell the roadie at the dressing room door to get lost.

Perhaps feeling bitter and twisted about being so untalented that he has to lug speakers around for a living, the roadie won't let me through, which means I am reduced to shagging the bass player who's also not allowed into the band's dressing room.

FRIDAY
1pm: The School Reunion

Hire unfeminine suit, corporate car plus a surprisingly cheap law degree from a high-brow university in order to impress my old pals from school at reunion lunch.

New boyfriend* not too impressed when I make him stay at home. However, I'm working under the assumption that I can't do a particularly convincing impression of a fabulously successful career woman if I'm seen to have a successful relationship too.

*See Thursday 9.30pm.

6pm: A Wine Bar

Drown my sorrows at a seedy bar in the city, trying to ignore the lascivious glances from all the old trendies who've turned off their mobiles just to make sure their menopausal wives don't call.

Every one of my bitch-cow, ex-private-school girlfriends turned up to the school reunion luncheon with their partners in tow which meant I had to sit at the end of the long table, well out of reach of the bottles of wine that were set in the middle of it.

Only comforted by the fact that none of them have particularly good jobs either and most of them looked suitably impressed by my Donna Karan suit.

7pm: The Office Party

Normally don't like to mix with my colleagues but figure that they can't bitch about my so-called aloof manner and snobbish ways if I actually deign to be in their presence for once.

Things don't get off to a particularly good start when my boss mistakes me for a gatecrasher and the cleaner catches me trying to clean the carpets with cheap and nasty red wine. While feeding the artificial pot plants with fertilizer masquerading as finger food, snub as many members of staff as possible without seeming rude or off-hand, top off my brief appearance by photocopying my new La Perla bra and then refusing to let any of my colleagues see it.

8.30pm: Classical Music Concert

Sit in grand, old, freezing-cold hall enduring a classical cacophony all the while cursing Beethoven for attempting to compose music while he was deaf. Daren't light up a Marlboro Light to calm my frazzled nerves, in case some evil spirit within me sees fit to lob lit matches at the woodwind section. After failing to catch the handsome second violinist's eye, and then getting ticked off by the conductor for shouting lustful intentions during the quiet bits, start frantically scanning my program for an end to my misery.

Dismayed to learn that I've got to sit in my best Chloe dress, through at least three more flute solos before the first interval.

10pm: The Cinema

Watch Hollywood's finest try to string two words together on screen while I'm attempting to open a packet of crisps in the dark. Annoying woman in the seat behind me tells me to shush, so on goes the gorgeous fur hat I bought on my last Moscow trip. Annoying man beside me asks if I could refrain from second-guessing the plot out loud – a case of sour grapes as I get it right every time.

Decide I've had enough when the people in front ask me to stop laughing hysterically during a poignant scene in which Gywneth Paltrow attempts to cry convincingly. Stomp off down the row of seats in my aisle, taking care not to avoid everyone's toes with my brand new Jimmy Choo heels.

11.30pm: A Nightclub

Barge straight to the front of the queue at a top new night-spot. In clearly-enunciated words, tell the squat, ugly bonehead at the door to get out of my way because I know the owner. In a cruel twist of fate, the squat, ugly bonehead *is* the owner and I'm escorted straight to the back of the line.

Two hours later, a disapproving hat-check girl takes my coat, no doubt jealous that it's genuine mink, so make her sign a sworn affidavit that I'll get the same one back at the end of the evening. Music is far too loud inside the club to make small talk so just do what all the other patrons do: stand against a wall and sneer. Sneer turns to snarl when I discover that the price of champagne would keep me in Gucci pants for a week. Upon seeing my distress, a male of Mediterranean descent slithers over and offers to buy me a drink.

Naturally, no man can buy my love but decide, on reflection, to get wretchedly drunk while he tries.

SATURDAY
11am: The Beach

Go to the beach to work on my skin melanoma which is currently in remission. Refuse to be put off by the sight of fat, pale, poor people hogging the sand and lay my towel close to the water's edge on top of an elaborate castle, complete with turrets, drawbridge and moat. Block my ears to the howls from under-age architects and block my nasal passages to avoid the stench of seaweed and sewerage.

Proceed to spend an enjoyable hour attempting to feed seagulls with the dirty syringes and broken glass that I find under my feet but get bored when a stranded seal pup starts gagging on the used condom it found in my bag.

1pm: The Races

Reluctantly agree to accompany a friend to a day at the races but only because I feel like wearing a hat. Do my bit to improve the image of arrogant French people by drinking vintage champagne in the VIP area.

Friend eventually asks why I haven't placed a bet or watched a race. Point out to her that if I wanted to watch vertically-challenged men do something exciting, I'd install gnomes in the grounds of my home.

3pm: The Football

Normally refuse to frequent any sports venue as a matter of feminine principle, but am feeling a bit pre-menstrual so make the effort to go in order to annoy my bass-playing boyfriend and cramp his style. Unimpressed with wasting my time watching such a ridiculous game, manage to rouse myself into a suitable state of football aggression. Impervious to boyfriend's pleas, throw Bolly bottles at players and tell hulking supporters to get an education.

End up stuck in casualty while boyfriend gets 132 stitches to his hands and face.

8pm The Dinner Party

Go to dinner party *sans* boyfriend – I don't want him bleeding over any vegetarian guests. Chat to the hostess in the kitchen. An overwhelming scent of garlic pervades the air, which forces me to eat all the after-dinner mints long before the starters are served. The meal is rather a subdued affair, particularly after I tell the hostess that I would have had the decency to retire to bed at the last minute with a sudden viral infection rather than serve up such a culinary debacle. To ensure that I don't overstay my welcome, the hostess starts serving coffee in the hallway while I collect my Gucci coat.

As I'm bundled out of the house, my mobile rings. A friend calls and begs me to accompany her to an S&M night at some squalid little dungeon. I decline, telling her that if I want to see a grown man in leathers, bleeding, crying and at the mercy of a girl who couldn't give a toss, I may as well go home to my convalescing boyfriend.

SUNDAY
11am: A Festival Gig

Reluctantly agree to join permanently-scarred boyfriend at a festival gig because I feel a mite guilty about the fact that he'll never be able to play the bass properly again.

Cannot understand why the great unwashed pay good money to stand in a muddy paddock waiting to use the portable loos. Also fail to see what is so alluring about sleeping under the stars – unless they allow you into their dressing rooms first (and boyfriend's band still won't let me in to see the lead singer).

After first torrential downpour and first act (making a worse din than usual, now that their bass player is plucking chords with his teeth), leave curt Dear John note with roadie, pick my way delicately passed the flailing fans in the mud, and head straight for the gate.

1pm: A Theatre Matinee

Upon hearing about my recent and traumatic relationship break-up, well-meaning friend tries to cheer me up by dragging me to see a new play that is the talk of the town. Of course, it's only being gossiped about because the lead actress has resorted to taking her clothes off to prop up the plot. Refuse to sit at the back of the theatre, because lone men in raincoats disturb me. Instead sit right up the front so I can ogle the main star's cellulite. During the interminable pauses, while she wrestles with buttons and zips, I give a running commentary on her physical flaws for the benefit of the short-sighted saps at the back. Could swear that lead actress is getting slightly annoyed but can't be totally sure as her expression never actually changes throughout.

4pm: A Tupperware Party

Attend as a favour to an artistic friend who is determined to collect an entire set of salad crispers for the sculpture of me that she is currently working on. Unfortunately, have to travel all the way to an outer suburb by cab, so don't arrive in the best of moods. Ignore all the other guests and survey the living room for something comforting and familiar – like style and good taste. The housewives sit around a Formica coffee table and ooh and aah while playing pass the parcel with pastel polyurethane. Politely refuse light refreshments, declaring that I'm allergic to processed cheese triangles and I don't do coffee that has been dry-frozen.

After purchasing her crispers and a couple of colanders, my friend whispers something in my ear about it being polite to place an order so that the hostess can get her bonus party gift. Put my name down for a miniature spatula and am pleased to note that the hostess now earns enough to qualify for a free plastic lid.

8pm: The Opera

Rue the day I agreed to become a patron of the arts. All the females on stage look like they've escaped from Weight Watchers and all the old women seated around me have unnaturally blue hair. Indeed, feel even more like a veritable goddess than usual in these less-than-picturesque surrounds. This thought comforts me little, though, as I have to also listen to non-English speaking Italians who sing like they've just spilt boiling Bolognese sauce down their trousers.

Tempted to hum along to the bits they've blatantly stolen from telly commercials, but have to leave before the first interval as my ears have started to bleed on to my new Versace dress.

Did You Know?

The only thing more embarrassing than asking a chemist for a packet of condoms is asking a record shop assistant for a Barry Manilow album.

5

BODY, SOUL &
BLOODY BAD
HAIR DAYS

5.1 DO MY BREASTS LOOK BIG IN THIS?

"The only place men want depth in a woman is in her décolletage."
Zsa Zsa Gabor

Men will do anything for a pretty face. Helen of Troy's beauty inspired them to go to war. She could have had the brain of a mollusc, the personality of a pigeon and the soul of a lamp-post for all they knew and they would still have died for her. However, you can be sure that had young Hellers been gorgeous from within but had the sort of face that could sink a thousand ships, her admirers would probably have stayed at home and polished their helmets instead. Men are shallow like that.

The Gorgons had to live down the fact that they were so ugly, one glance at a man could turn him to stone. Then there was poor plump and plain Anne of Cleves. Starting the trend that now sees rich and famous men book their girlfriends through modelling agencies, Henry VIII spotted a highly-flattering painting of Anne, and decided to marry her. When he met her in the flesh and found out that – unlike the camera – the artist often lies, he got an annulment pronto.

It's not surprising then that men's wholesale worship of beauty inspires bad behaviour. Why act like a saint when you look like an angel? Why be punctilious, courteous, modest, meek and mild if you're a natural-born stunner? Who's going to tell off a goddess? And what's the bet that women's prisons are full of plain people?

Everybody knows that girls with woeful figures and milk-curdling faces don't get away with murder whereas the Pamela Anderson prototype could bludgeon her grandma's budgie to death and still get let off with a gentle chiding from the RSPCA.

Ways to tell if you're attractive

- You get whistled at by building-site workers.
- Men want to sleep with you.
- Girls want to sleep with you.
- Men rush up to you in the street with large bouquets of flowers.
- Girls want to be your friend.
- Men declare wars on neighbouring countries to impress you.
- Girls bitch behind your back about the fact that they've lost fathers, sons, brothers and uncles all thanks to you.
- Men are nice to you for no good reason.
- Girls are nasty to you for no good reason.
- Men go red when they speak to you.
- Girls go green when they see you.
- Men won't ask you out because they assume you're already taken.
- Girls won't be seen with you because you're too much competition.
- Cabs stop for you immediately, even if they're already taken.
- Moving cars screech to a halt the moment you step on to a pedestrian crossing.
- No-one ever forgets your name.
- People are always mistaking you for Cameron Diaz.
- Old men offer to open doors for you.
- Old ladies offer to carry your bags for you.
- Pregnant women give up their seats for you on trains and buses.
- Policemen tear up your speeding tickets.
- Other girls clutch on to their boyfriends the moment you enter the room.
- You always get the job, even when you didn't apply for it.
- You always get let off on murder charges.

Beauty Spot

If you're sick of being judged by your looks and would infinitely prefer to look like Elephant Man's less attractive daughter, try bathing in a vat of acid.

CAN YOU TURN THE LIGHTS DOWN PLEASE?

How To Look Good Against All Odds

No-one – except girls with good make-up artists, great lighting technicians, and fantastic airbrush artists – can drink like a fish, smoke like a chimney, tan like a Hereford cow, eat like a very small hamster and expect not to need a little cosmetic enhancement. Unfortunately, most bad girls can't be fagged to spend six hours in the bathroom each morning just so that they can look like they haven't been on a bender the night before. Nor can they afford to spend squillions on miracle anti-aging creams that only ever seem to work on the 13-year-old models endorsing them. However, with a little bit of cunning and a lot of short-cuts, you too can look fresh, vibrant and youthful in any light (so long as the dimmers are on and you're wearing a net curtain over your head).

Beauty in a hurry
- Use talcum powder as dry shampoo when there's no time to wash your hair.
- Use roll-on deodorant and perfume in lieu of having a bath.
- Peel-off blackhead plasters in lieu of having to wash your face.

- Wear ladder-proof tights rather than shave your legs.
- Fix holes in ladder-proof tights with clear nail polish.
- Set yesterday's make-up with translucent powder.
- Cover running eye-liner smudges with concealer.
- Wear dark glasses to hide concealer.

Beauty on a budget

- Make the most of organic, all-natural, fruit-based or vegetable-based face peels by eating the left-overs.
- A brisk rub with a Brillo pad will ensure that your skin has a natural glow.
- An accidental squirt of hairspray towards your face will ensure your eyes naturally sparkle.
- Biting all your nails off is cheaper than manicuring them.
- To get your money's worth out of a waterproof mascara, always remember to fall into a nearby swimming pool.
- Stuffing tissues down your bra is cheaper than surgical implants and is handy when you suddenly come down with a cold.
- To receive your complimentary make-up bag with free lipstick, mascara, tweezers and bubble bath – buy the extortionately priced product you need to receive it, then return the product at a later date for a full refund.
- If shop-lifting makes you feel bad, only steal sale items then the retailer can claim the item's full value on the insurance.

Fair Comment

Marilyn Monroe was living proof that blondes don't always have more fun (particularly if they take up with a Kennedy).

DON'T HATE ME BECAUSE I'M GORGEOUS

Grooming Etiquette For Very Vain Girls

If you have got the time and the money, you might like to let the experts cut, colour, shape, shade, style, tweeze and squeeze your best features into something remotely presentable. Your superior grooming will be appreciated by all and sundry, except the poor suckers responsible for doing it.

Brushing hair stylists up the wrong way

- Demand fresh ashtrays, magazines and cups of coffee every five minutes.
- Thwart their artistic pretensions by demanding a trim.
- Start to cry as soon as you see the end result in the mirror.

Causing ugly scenes at the beauty salon

- Tell the beautician you can't stand new age music and can she put some death metal on instead.
- Emit ear-piercing shrieks every time she attempts to pluck a single hair from your brow, chin or bikini line.
- Make her jealous by saying you rarely cleanse, tone or moisturize and you never take off your make-up before going to bed.

Turning the tables on make-up counter mavens

- Lean over the counter, give her a scrutinizing look and say "Hmmm. I'd say you've got prematurely aging skin with a couple of oily patches."
- Tell her you want something to make you look as old as she does because you're sick of being mistaken for a teenager.
- Test 58 shades of red lipstick – on *her* hand instead of yours.

Tearing snotty sales assistants to shreds

- Unfold all sweaters, cardigans and jumpers on shelves to check sizes and styles.
- Try on at least 15 pairs of shoes before tossing them all carelessly aside and walking out of shop.
- Try on a blouse, get lipstick all over it and then demand a discount because it's stained.

New Commandment
Don't covet thy neighbour's ass. It's probably been liposuctioned.

MY LIFE AS A STARTLED RABBIT

An Intimate Guide To Cosmetic Surgery

Mercifully lacking up-close operation pictures, and cleverly avoiding obviously doctored before and after shots, this distressing account from an anonymous patient guides you through the perils of invasive surgery in the hope that you, at least, can come out of it in one fairly attractive piece.

Liposuction

Before: Couldn't fit into designer trousers. Fat reduction seemed cheaper alternative to buying another pair in size 10.

After: Using pair of crutches, had to hobble to shops to buy designer trousers in size 10 because still couldn't fit into original size 8, thanks to compression bandages I had to wear for weeks after the operation.

Tummy Tuck

Before: After leg swellings went down, finally managed to fit into size 8 designer trousers but couldn't do the zip up.

After: Couldn't wear the trousers for months as tummy far too sore to be touched by anything.

Breast Enlargement

Before: After weeping stomach wounds finally healed, bought matching low-cut single-breasted jacket to go with size 8 trousers but discovered that cleavage didn't do the jacket justice.

After: Husband refused to speak to me after one new breast started to leak on the bedclothes.

Facelift

Before: Wanted to publicly embarrass husband for being so shallow and superficial about breast enlargement ordeal.

After: Managed to publicly embarrass husband by refusing to wear sunglasses and a headscarf to disguise black eyes, stitches and spasmodic bleeding.

Ear Correction

Before: As a result of the facelift needed to have ears lowered by two centimetres.

After: Lobes too tender to wear earrings that were bought to complement designer trousers and matching low-cut single-breasted jacket.

Eye Improvement

Before: In need of a boost after depressing after-effects of ear correction surgery.

After: Once pain subsided and bruises cleared, husband declared that I looked like a startled rabbit.

Cosmetic Dentistry

Before: Taking husband's rabbit comments seriously, decided to get buck teeth fixed.

After: With a mouthful of large, even, white teeth, husband said I looked like a horse.

Rhinoplasty

Before: Opted for getting nose re-shaped in order to look less horse-like.

After: When nose had finally stopped bleeding, saw results in mirror and realized why Michael Jackson always travels in disguise.

Chin Tuck

Before: Got sick of wearing extremely high-necked sweater to hide botched nose job.

After: Had to wear high-necked sweater to hide black and blue chin.

Neck Lift

Before: By the time I could safely discard high-necked sweater and wear low-cut single-breasted jacket again, realized that neck had aged considerably.

After: Following neck lift, discovered two boils above jaw-line.

Dermabrasion

Before: Decided to get skin sand-blasted after being informed by another cosmetic surgeon that the boils on my jawline were in fact my nipples.

After: Husband left me for a home-wrecker who was a natural size 8.

Please note: Should extensive cosmetic surgery prove beyond your budget, borrow the money from a friend or family member. Hopefully, if the surgeon does the job properly, you won't have to pay the loan back as no-one will recognize you.

Other attractive forms of self-mutilation

Body Piercings Multiple earrings are great to fiddle with in order to annoy other people; Nipple rings are great to hang spare sets of keys; tummy rings are great for encouraging men to contemplate your navel; genital rings are great for discouraging men who have metal allergies.

Spectacles Fantastic way to appear intelligent when you're not, by driving men off in droves.

Coloured Contact Lenses Perfect for scaring away small animals and children; also ideal if you've just landed the lead role in *Idiot Alien From Planet Dweeb*.

Tattoos A more down-market form of body art: you look like someone's taken to you with a biro.

Body Art A more up-market form of tattooing – you look like someone's taken to you with a paint brush.

Branding Performed upon woolly-brained women instead of sheep. Cigarettes and irons are a cheap alternative.

Decoration Tip
Braces are an excellent way to enhance your scowl.

SHIT, I'VE JUST BURNT MY WONDERBRA

Hard Lessons For Style Vultures And Fashion Victims

Most women dress for women which is great news for the small group of females who prefer to get a shag instead. Not for us black sheep, the slavish trends and ridiculous fads that make all girls look like mutant clones and make all men secretly yearn for old-fashioned fish-net tights and totally uncool short black fan-belts. Bad girls wear Spandex boob-tubes and nine-inch stilettos whether they're outré or not. And while other women might look at them sidewards and sneer, you can guarantee men will look at them straight on and swoon.

Sundry item

Only buy gloves, hats, belts, watches, sunglasses and scarves if you want to lose them.

Clothes that act as your own personal chaperon

- Skirts that stop at the knees or mid-calf.
- Skirts that go further than the top of your thigh.
- Knitwear that makes you look like your mother.
- Tracksuits that make you look like your brother.
- Linen (unless you want to look like something that's just been picked up off the floor).
- Wedding veils.
- Wedding dresses.
- Tights with unsightly toe seams.
- Tights in any colour other than black or tan.

- White stilettos with black tights.
- Skin-coloured underwear.
- Fleece-lined sweatshirts.
- Non-visible panty line.
- Expensive dresses posing as bohemian tat.
- Jeans that are ripped or torn when you buy them.
- Yashmaks.
- Berets.
- Bustles.
- Mittens.
- Flip-flops.
- Sarongs.
- Ear muffs.
- Crinolines.
- Foot-binding.
- Neck rings.
- Sports bras.
- Pearls.

Ideal Washing Instructions

Do not machine wash. Do not hand wash. Do not dry clean. Do not tumble dry. Do not hang up or fold flat to dry. Do not iron. Simply pick up off floor or take out of laundry basket, put on and then, if needed, give a bit of a spit wash before leaving the house.

PINK IS FOR PRATS

A Colour Chart For The Colour Blind

Red Makes you look like a giant blood clot.

Orange Brings out the natural redness in cheeks, nose and eyeballs alike. Only advisable if you're a clean-living Hare Krishna sort.

Yellow Apparently the colour most likely to incite vandalism when used to coat the walls in public toilets.

Pink Even flamingos can't be taken seriously wearing this colour.

Green Mother Nature's registered trademark, and the sworn enemy of bad girls. Also comes in *Khaki* which is handy if you ever find yourself stuck up a tree, and *Chartreuse*, a revolting off-lime green colour which doesn't look good on any girl, bad or otherwise.

Blue Supposed to promote feelings of tranquility and good-will which is strange considering it's also the preferred colour of air stewards, bank tellers and the police force.

Indigo A browny-purply-blacky colour that only looks good on an aubergine.

Violet Term used *ad nauseum* to describe the amazing colour of Elizabeth Taylor's eyes.

Brown Avoid at all costs unless you can afford subtle and varying shades in leather, suede or cashmere, or unless you enjoy being mistaken for an over-aged Brownie.

Cream The bad-but-honest girl's version of white on her wedding day.

White Suggests purity of mind, body and soul. Also suggests sallow or pallid complexions.

Grey Horrible hue that doesn't even suit nubile schoolgirls or pre-pubescent models.

Black The only shade worth wearing because it hides a multitude of sins, from uneven and highly unfair distribution of fat to the fact that you can't be bothered to mix and match your clothes in the morning.

I HAVEN'T GOT A SINGLE THING TO WEAR

Good Reasons For Walking Around Naked

1. *The weather's getting better.*

2. *There's a man you want to impress at work.*

3. *All your clothes got burnt in a fire.*

4. *You're waiting for the sales to start.*

5. *No-one will know how much money you earn.*

6. *No-one will know whether you've got style or not.*

7. *No-one will ask you where you bought your skirt.*

8. *No-one will ask you how much it cost.*

9. *No-one will ask to borrow it.*

10. *No-one will race out and buy the same one.*

11. *You look better undressed.*

12. *You look worse undressed but you're a committed naturalist.*

Top Tip
Press your work clothes in the morning by standing in a tightly packed train.

5.2 BURNING TOAST IS BURNING CALORIES, ISN'T IT?

*"I am anorexic actually. Anorexic people look in the mirror
and think they're fat. So do I."*
Jo Brand

As you idly flick through the pages of this book, you may notice that
the following section seems rather short in comparison to others. Well,
what do you expect when the subject's about keeping fit and eating
well?

This is a guide to achieving the body beautiful *without* having to
resort to drastic measures such as a balanced diet and regular exercise. Why count calories when you're going to eat them anyway? Why
bother jogging when you plan upon moaning every single step of the
way.

Therefore the only topics worth including here are eating disorders
and frenetic sex. And if you're a bad girl, you probably know quite a
bit about both of them already.

Dietary Aid
To appear slimmer, always hang out with fat friends.

I'LL TAKE THE SNICKERS, THANKS

Is Chocolate Better Than Sex?

This is an age-old argument. Is a glass-and-a-half of full-cream milk better than two teaspoons of something that simply looks like full-cream milk? To settle the debate once and for all, a self-sacrificing female (who wishes to remain anonymous) measures man against the cocoa bean and reports back on her findings:

1. *Have an argument with my boyfriend in supermarket when I catch him trying to put diet white chocolate into the trolley when he knows I can't stand the stuff.*

2. *Buy bitter-sweet, dark chocolate bar to console myself when he storms off and leaves me alone in the confectionery aisle.*

3. *Drive chocolate bar home, taking note of the fact that it doesn't nag me for turning right from the left-hand lane.*

4. *Once home, stare longingly at the phone while waiting for boyfriend to call to apologize.*

5. *Get bored after ten minutes so start staring longingly at chocolate bar.*

6. *Chocolate bar seems attractive in a dark and silent sort of way.*

7. *Start talking to myself while still staring longingly at chocolate bar.*

8. *Unlike my boyfriend, chocolate bar listens.*

9. *Start pouring out my feelings to chocolate bar.*

10. *Chocolate bar doesn't interrupt with its own tales of infinitely more superior woes.*

11. *Tell chocolate bar that boyfriend doesn't understand me.*

12. *Chocolate bar seems to nod in agreement though this could be the fact that it's now late at night and I've had quite a bit to drink.*

13. *Shyly ask chocolate bar if I can eat it.*

14. *Chocolate bar winks in collusion though this could be moonlight hitting the shiny packaging.*

15. *Which reminds me, chocolate bars dress better than my boyfriend.*

16. *Thank the lord that it's a bitter-sweet chocolate bar rather than a sickly sweet one because, quite frankly, sweet chocolate tastes revolting when you drink it with alcohol.*

17. *Lick, nibble and finally gobble chocolate bar, all the while worrying about my cellulite.*

18. *Left feeling sated but ripped off because chocolate bar wasn't one of those ten-per-cent-extra-at-no-extra-cost chocolate bars.*

19. *Boyfriend rings to apologize about his disgraceful behaviour in the supermarket.*

20. *Chuck chocolate bar wrapper in bin, wipe tell-tale stains from face and wait for boyfriend to come around and shag me because I'm allowed to have both, aren't I?*

Desperate measure
Refuse to adhere to the old adage "If it tastes good, spit it out." Indeed, if it tastes good, swallow it. Then spit it out.

MY BOWELS REALLY CAN'T STOMACH THIS

Using Allergies To Avoid Eating Horrible Food

- Start hyperventilating every time someone serves up or cous-cous.
- Break out in a rash whenever you walk past a health food shop.
- Choke on a fish cake.
- Pass out if a restaurant waiter takes your order from you within 30 minutes.
- Cringe whenever a spotty-faced youth asks if you'd like fries with that.
- Scream when you find a hairnet in your hamburger.
- Begin shivering when a barman spikes your scotch and coke with ice.
- Throw up if you see anyone eating haggis.

AN APPLE A DAY KEEPS MY WORRIES AT BAY

Eating Disorders Made Alarmingly Easy

- Feel starved of affection, attention or control for whatever the reason.
- Feel fat because of it for some strange reason.
- Learn the exact calorie content of every food item known to mankind.
- Never eat in public but smile a lot.
- Always binge in private and cry a lot.
- Eat nothing – because you're full up on that piece of apple you ate two days ago.
- Eat every food item known to mankind – in one sitting. Alone.
- Stand on your bathroom scales whenever you can.
- Stare into full-length mirrors whenever you can.
- Tell everyone you think you're fat.
- Privately think everyone else is fat.
- Wonder why it's mostly women who worry about being fat.
- Wonder why it's mostly men, or your mother, who tell you that you're fat.
- Wear clothes to emphasize your thinness.
- Tell everyone you're putting on weight to stop all their nagging.
- Wear clothes to hide your thinness.
- Dash to the toilet straight after eating.
- Deny to your family that you've got an eating disorder.
- Deny to your shrink that you've got an eating disorder.
- Scream at the nurses for making you eat.
- Resent all the other patients because they're thinner than you.
- Tell the world press that you had an eating disorder but that

you're getting much better.

- Tell yourself that you're getting much better.
- Eat the rest of the apple you started all those days ago.

I CAN'T EAT ANYTHING GROWN IN THE GROUND

Upsetting The Apple-Cart At Mealtimes

- Strain freshly squeezed orange juice to get rid of the pulp.
- Pick the hazelnuts, raisins, sultanas, oatmeal, bran flakes, dried apple and weevils out of your bowl of muesli.
- Faint at the sight of a blood-red tomato.
- Feed broccoli, cauliflower and brussel sprouts to the host's vegetarian dog sitting under the table.
- Flick peas at very young guests.

Why Don't You?
Refuse to become a vegetarian because it's cruel to butchers.

SEX IS EXERCISE, ISN'T IT?

Why Bad Girls Prefer To Get Their Kit Off

Life is all about sex and who's going to have sex with you if you've got arms the size of your thighs and thighs the size of a man's? Men feel threatened enough without you trying to outdo them in the inside-leg measurement department.

Despite the discouraging sights seen on tennis courts, hockey pitches and gym mats, there are some short-sighted optimists who maintain that girls who engage in rigorous exercise can look sexy. Look at, um, you know. Whatserface. The one who ran off with that other female wrestler.

Let's get real here – girls playing sport look appealing so long as you don't stand them anywhere near a girl who doesn't play sport. The only good thing about wielding racquets or taking steroids is that you might end up with a million-pound sponsorship deal. Since we're working under the assumption that you don't know your backhand from your forearm, and wouldn't recognize a StairMaster machine even if you tripped over one, we're going to have to find you another way to work up a sweat.

The alternative exercise plan:

- Stay in bed and have sex more often.

Energy-Saving Tip
If you find sex exhausting, you're obviously doing it wrong.

5.3 GO TELL IT TO FLORENCE NIGHTINGALE

"You go to a psychiatrist when you're slightly cracked and keep going until you're completely broke."
Joan Rivers

If you want to learn more about your mental state of health, check out this section's sympathetic and sensitive portrayal of drink and drugs and how best to seek them out. Likewise, if you wish to make the most of madness and melancholia, don't miss our essential guide to women on the verge of feigning a nervous breakdown.

However, if you need to know all about causes, symptoms and cures for diseases, infections, viruses, growths, carbuncles, boils, and irritable bowel syndrome, then read something else.

While their nerves might be shot to pieces by having to deal with sick partners and the medical profession, bad girls never suffer from physical ill health. They're the carriers of bugs, germs and bad news, not the dumping grounds. And they certainly never have the time to be struck down with a life-threatening illness since they're far too busy dreaming up radical and alternative remedies to put paid to all the hypochondriacs and ghouls that surround them.

Behaving badly at the doctor's

- While picking up your prescription for the Pill, mention to your doctor that you've got a locked jaw, a dry throat, a back ache, a stomach ache, a runny nose, sore eyes, stiff joints, blurred vision, ringing in your ears, hives, piles, eczema, asthma, acne, the runs, worms, shingles, chilblains, varicose veins, external bruising, internal bleeding, mysterious cysts, and a tense and nervous headache.

- Feign surprise and gob-smacked awe when he knowledgeably tells you that the symptoms are all caused by stress.

- Feign a little less surprise and gob-smacked awe when he prescribes you with a course of antibiotics.

Behaving badly at the hospital

- While waiting in casualty to get a couple of aspirin for a light headache, stab yourself firmly in the chest in order to jump the queue.

- During open-heart surgery, sit up in bed suddenly, while you're meant to be under anaesthetic, and ask the incompetents around you why they aren't using rubber gloves.

- After your operation, demand that the nurse shaves your head in the hope that you too may be visited by a caring, sharing celebrity or get a free trip to Disneyland.

Behaving badly at the dentist's

- Start how your dentist intends to go on and greet him at reception with a cheery "Phnar, phnarfalll, whaff, arghthph-rnghh, prhraff"*.

- When you've finished swilling your mouthwash at the end of dental procedures, accidentally spit it out at the idiot nurse for deliberately drenching your clothes with the water spray.

- Take out a pair of pliers from your handbag, rip your new fillings out of your mouth and hurl them at the receptionist as soon as you see the size of your bill.

*Loosely translated as "My teeth are perfectly fine but as it's my annual check-up and you're my money-grubbing dentist, you may as well give me the fillings I neither want or need".

Behaving badly at the optician's

- Send all his expensive equipment flying as you stumble into the room.

- Subliminally abuse him for extortionate prices for tiny pieces of plastic by misreading the letters on the eye chart in the following order: "U", "R", "A", "F", "N", "C".

- Deliberately drop both of your extortionately-priced tiny pieces of plastic on the floor so he has to waste valuable charging time looking for them.

Good Point

How come you can't find Get Well cards with printed inscriptions that run along the lines of: "Sorry to hear you might be dying...can I have your house if you do?"

QUIT YOUR MOANING AND GAG ON THIS

Bedside Manners To Apply To Malingering Partners

While many student nurses will rave about how truly wonderful Florence Nightingale was for devoting her life to looking after sick and wounded soldiers during the Crimean War, some of us less compassionate, females secretly think she should have been taken out of the medical tent and shot. Not least because she single-handedly turned all men into the raving hypochondriacs they are today.

If your partner's trying to extract the milk of human kindness from you by pretending to be infected, diseased or injured, give him something a little less palatable to ensure he never pulls such a stupid stunt again.

Chicken Noodle Soup Add boiling water to one packet of two-minute instant noodles. Toss in cauldron with partially frozen chicken pieces. Stir vigorously until noodles are soft. Serve immediately.

Hearty Beef Drink Boil British beef on the bone. Pour extracts into mug. Serve as often as required until patient is mooing in a maniacal manner.

Meals on Wheels Take any ready-prepared meal, well past its use-by-date, and heat according to instructions. Put in the fridge for several more days and then reheat it again. Place on trolley, wheel to appropriate bedroom and serve with bright, fake smile.

Comfort Food Unwrap packet of six pork sausages. Leave on breadboard overnight (with central heating on High). Chop and dice carrots, onions and potatoes on the same breadboard the following morning. Lob the lot in casserole dish and simmer in oven until sausages are slightly warm. Serve in mock-caring manner.

I WANT TO BE BURIED WITH MY ASHES

Quitting Smoking Even If It Kills You

1. *Stop all activities which may trigger your desire to smoke (waking up, stretching, yawning, getting out of bed, having a bath, drinking coffee, eating breakfast, waiting for the bus, reading, writing, working, talking on the telephone, talking to people, talking to yourself, going down the pub after work, drinking alcohol, starting a meal, eating a meal, finishing a meal, watching telly, thinking about having sex, having sex, relaxing after having had sex).*

2. *Keep yourself occupied by only doing those activities not mentioned above (showering and sleeping).*

3. *Fly direct to Texas, America – on a non-smoking flight, naturally.*

4. *Deliberately, and with cold-blooded intent, murder a passing Texan.*

5. *Take the electric chair.*

Other less final ways to give up smoking

Nicotine Chewing Gum Too tempting to chew gum and smoke cigarettes simultaneously for that double-whammy rush.

Nicotine Patch Ideal for covering up the skin rashes it usually causes.

Nicotine Inhaler It sort of looks like a cigarette. You can hold it like you would a cigarette. It gives you doses of highly-addictive nicotine just like a cigarette. So why bloody bother?

Hypnosis Expensive way of falling asleep for 45 minutes.

Acupuncture Only good if acupuncturist sticks a needle in your eye so you can't actually find your way to the tobacconist.

Nagging Partner The least effective method of the lot since his nagging will make you so stressed out that you'll probably smoke even more. Either that or you'll resort to puffing away behind his back which, in turn, means you'll probably drop him so you can get more cigarette breaks in.

Sobering Thought

If a man attempts to get you drunk, you're obviously not doing a good enough job of it by yourself.

GIVE ME THAT BEER OR I'LL RIP YOUR HORNS OFF

The Devil's Brew And How To Get It Off Him

There's a lot to be said for developing a drink problem. You can blame all your problems on one thing. You don't have to remember all the stupid things you said and did the night before. And you never need a man to lean on when there's a perfectly good bar counter nearby.

On the down side though, you'll never be able to write your autobiography because you'll never be able to remember what you've done. You'll ring up ex-lovers at three o'clock in the morning under the mistaken impression that they're dying to hear from you. And you'll have to lie when you fill in medical questionnaires.

What medical questionnaires should really ask you

1. *How much do you drink on average per week?*
   a. *The recommended limit of 14-21 units per week.*
   b. *Is a unit the same as a bottle?*
   c. *A small wine glass or a single measure of spirits is a unit, you say? Well, sod that for a lark.*

2. *Have you every woken up*
   a. *Thinking it's good to be alive?*
   b. *Lying in a strange man's bed?*
   c. *Lying in a strange gutter, in a strange town, in a strange country, wondering why the strange policeman is looking down at you, strangely?*

3. *Do you ever worry that you have a drinking problem*
   a. *No. Of course not.*
   b. *Well, I'm hardly going to admit it to you, now am I?*
   c. *No. Why? Do you? I've heard that doctors are complete and utter pissheads.*

4. *Do you ever drink alone?*
   a. *No. Never.*
   b. *Yes, but only because there's no-one else around to have a drink with.*
   c. *Yes, but only when there's no-one else around to have a drink with.*

The New Improved 2-Step AA Program

Step 1: *Stand up and say, "My name is [insert name here] and I am a member of the AA".*

Step 2: *Then say, "However, I may cancel my membership soon as I plan to sell my car and buy a bicycle."*

A few drastic hangover measures

A car crash Works on the theory that one excrutiating pain can distract from another, rather than just making you feel twice as bad.

A hair of the dog Dangerous, short-term remedy, mainly because you could end up catching fleas.

A death in the family A marvellous, though perhaps inconvenient, means of making all your own problems instantly appear rather trivial.

A fried breakfast When you start to retch at the sight of it, you may also get rid of some excess alcohol.

Plenty of water Only successful if you are well enough to manage to drown yourself in it.

Alternative highs for insatiable drug fiends

- Attending book readings, watching political broadcasts or forgetting to close your gas-oven door all serve as excellent and perfectly legal narcotics.
- Giving up a diet, quitting the dating game or taking up smoking again all act as effective anti-depressants.
- Eating instant coffee straight from the jar or having a knock-down-drag-out fight with your partner both serve as great stimulants.
- An emergency service responding at the first ring provides the same effect as a tranquilizer.
- The sudden death of someone you loathe is a brilliant mood-enhancer.

Mental Note
If you think you're constantly being watched or followed, take the unpaid-for item back from out of your bag and discreetly pop it back on to the shelf.

I'M FRIGHTENED OF MY TOILET BRUSH

Feigning Phobias Made Easy

Any bad girl who goes to see a shrink needs her head examined. You don't need some patronizing professional to tell you that you're as mad as a mad cow with mad cow's disease. You should know that already. However, if you don't think you're quite neurotic enough, why not stage a good old-fashioned panic attack and feign a phobia? That way you can use your unfounded but abject terror to avoid unpleasant people, places or tasks.

Fear of Open Spaces
- Inability to see the attraction of large, open-air rock concerts.
- Refusal to venture into the countryside.
- Aversion to supermarkets (so that you have to shop at corner shops instead).

Fear of Enclosed Spaces
- Inability to parallel park.
- Refusal to use public phone boxes or public toilets.
- Aversion to being pinned down to the mattress by your lover.

Fear of Animals
- Reluctance to donate to the World Wildlife Fund.
- Refusal to walk anywhere in case you step in dog dung.
- Aversion to pet hair on clothes, couches and car seats.

Fear of Heights

- Reluctance to ascend flight of stairs when there's a nearby lift in perfectly good working order.
- Inability to dust anything that's on a table, shelf, cabinet, mantle piece or window sill.
- Aversion to climbing out of bed in the morning.

Fear of Fire

- Inability to light your own cigarettes when good-looking men are around.
- Impulse to rip-out authentic fireplace and replace it with a cleaner, more efficient gas heater.
- Refusal to enter a burning building.

Fear of Water

- Reluctance to drink anything that comes out of a tap.
- Refusal to jump into a pool to save a drowning child on account of the fact that you don't want to get your hair wet.
- Aversion to washing dishes.

Fear of Flying

- Inability to face concept of boarding long-haul flights without being completely maggotted first.
- Impulse to shoot pigeons.
- Aversion to drugs that make you think you can fly when you jump from tall buildings.

Fear of Germs

- Reluctance to pick up a toilet brush and clean the toilet.
- Aversion to staying in hospital wards.
- Refusal to shake hands with estate agents, car salesmen or tax inspectors.

Fear of Failure

- Tendency to lie, cheat or steal while playing Scruples, Scrabble or Monopoly.
- Aversion to taking driving tests, pregnancy tests and blood tests.
- Refusing to open packets of dry roasted peanuts with your bare hands.

Fear of Commitment

- Inability to fancy a man who wants a long-term relationship with you.
- Aversion to mortgages, gym subscriptions and mobile phone contracts.
- Reluctance to make New Year's resolutions.

Fear of Getting Old

- Aversion to birthdays.
- Inability to act your age.
- Tendency to date only very young men.

Fear of God

- Reluctance to open the door when a Jehovah's Witness is behind it.
- Tendency to feel guilty about something you did even when no-one saw you do it.
- Aversion to swearing on your mother's life when you've just been caught out in a lie.

The above-mentioned phobias are the more common ones you can affect. However, other rarer cases of extreme fear abound. For instance, you can also suffer from

Fear of Hard Work.

Fear of Bedside Alarm Clocks.

Fear of The Tax Man.

Fear of Traffic Wardens.

Fear of Parking Tickets.

Fear of Policemen Looking Younger Than You.

Fear of Other People's Holiday Snaps.

Fear of Other People's Mobile Phones.

Fear of Running Out Of Cigarettes.

Fear of Match-Making Friends.

Fear of Vending Machines Thieving Your Money.

Fear of Genetically Modified Food.

Fear of Luke-Warm Food Sitting In Bain-Maries.

Fear of Leaving The Iron On When You Leave The House.

Fear of Unlimited Store Cards.

Fear of Bank Charges.

Fear of Born-Again Christians.

Fear of Big Issue Sellers.

Fear of Shopping Trolleys.
Fear of Old People Stopping You to Chat.
Fear of Bank Tellers Stopping For Lunch Before You Get To The Counter.
Fear of Home Gym Equipment.
Fear of Extremely Long Lists Like This One.

Mad Gesture

Who needs an expensive shrink when your mother will dish out advice for free?

OH GOSH, I DIDN'T MEAN TO MAKE YOU BLEED

How To Act Pre-Menstrual Even When You're Not

When you think about it, it's a bit of a bugger that pre-menstrual tension comes but once a month. Who wants to be reined in by hormones when you could act like a raving loon seven days a week? Why only get one stab at upsetting your partner when you could take to him with a bread knife around the clock? And how come men blame hysterical outbursts and unreasonable behaviour on your period, even when you're not having it?

Why all girls should have permanent PMT

- You can yell at shop assistants without feeling bad about it.
- You can cry in front of your boss and embarrass him.
- You can eat a family-sized box of chocolate without pausing to chew.
- You can blame weight gain on bloating and fluid retention.
- You can burn dinner.
- You can threaten to kill your partner when he refuses to eat it.
- You can kill your partner when he refuses to take your threat seriously.
- You can cry in front of the jury.
- You can scream abuse at the judge.
- You can plead diminished responsibility on the grounds that you were severely pre-menstrual at the time of the crime.
- You can usually get away with a good-behaviour bond.
- You can start the whole process again in 28 days.

Conversation with a woman on the edge

MAN   *Hi, honey. I'm home.*

WOMAN   (SNARLS) Fuck off and die, arsehole.

MAN   *Oh, I say. That wasn't very friendly.*

WOMAN   (BURSTS INTO TEARS) Oh, sorry. Please forgive me. I
          don't know what came over me.

MAN   *That time of the month, huh?*

WOMAN   (CRYING STOPS...SOUND OF EYES NARROWING) What
          do you mean by *that*?

MAN   *Nothing, nothing.*

WOMAN   No, come on, sheep-for-brains. You're obviously spoiling
          for a fight.

MAN   *No, I'm not.*

WOMAN   Yes, you are. Dog-breath.

MAN   *No, I'm not.*

WOMAN   Oh, so it's *my* fault then is it, you evil-eyed weasel?

MAN   *No, I'm just saying...*

WOMAN   (INTERRUPTING) See! Just like I was just saying. You
          never listen to *me*. It's always you, you, you.

MAN   *No, it's...*

WOMAN   Then how come you didn't call me, you lying, cheating,
          scumbag?

MAN   *Call you when?*

WOMAN   That time three and a half years ago when you said that
          you would.

MAN   *Huh?*

WOMAN   See, you're so selfish you can't even remember...
          toad-shagging poisonous little dwarf.

MAN   *I...*

WOMAN   Well, that's it. I'm not putting up with your emotional
          abuse any longer, you useless little worm. Get out of this
          house before I kill you. (SOUND OF KNIFE BEING
          BRANDISHED) Now!

MAN   *Okay, if you insist...*

WOMAN   (REACHING HYSTERIA) And come back here when I'm
          talking to you!

MAN   *But...*

WOMAN   (BURSTS INTO TEARS AGAIN) Come back. Come back.
          I didn't mean it. I'm so sorry.

MAN   *(SOOTHING TONES) That's okay, honey. Of course,*
          I forgive you.

WOMAN   (CRYING STOPS. SOUND OF EYES NARROWING) You
          forgive *me*? I thought we'd agreed it was all your fault?

MAN   *(SOUND OF HIM ROLLING HIS EYES)*

Hormonal Hint

To make the best of a bad deal during that time of the month,
catch up with those people who get on your nerves even when
you aren't feeling pre-menstrual.

5.4 THE PHILISTINE'S PROPHECY

"If only we'd stop trying to be happy we could have a pretty good time."
Edith Wharton

As one millennium leaves and another one arrives, it's time for more soul-searching and navel-gazing than ever before. So go on. Take a long, hard look at yourself and then answer me this. Do you honestly want to be perceived as a shallow, superficial, thrill-seeking, good-time party girl who couldn't give a stuff about her interior life?

I'll be relieved but not massively surprised if your answer is a resounding "Yes". You, of all people know that while a few seaweed supplements and a couple of hideously expensive inner-woman work-shops might solve all your problems, a gallon of decent wine or a bitch session with friends is usually far more effective.

So here's an alternative guide to alternative living. Here's a controversial take on holistic healings and ancient teachings to study fervently and practise fanatically – just so all the new-age nutters around you can say, with some authority and with a lot of feeling, that you really are a spiritual philistine.

How to change your life in seven days

Day One Quit smoking.
Day Two Quit drinking.
Day Three Quit eating red meat, sugar, salt, and smoked, fatty or highly refined foods.
Day Four Quit gratuitous sex.

Day Five Quit listening to loud music while driving a very fast, petrol-guzzling sports car.

Day Six Quit watching The Jerry Springer Show.

Day Seven Stick your head in the oven.

Further non-essential reading

Women Are From Heaven, Men Are From Hell

Women Who Run With Wolves And Decide They Make Much Better Pets Than Men

The Fire Within And How To Put It Out Without Soaking Your New Carpets

Women Who Love Too Much And Women Who Couldn't Give A Toss

Discovering The Child Within And Telling It Off For Wetting Its Nappy

How To Win Friends And Influence People Without Having To Buy Them A Single Drink

I'm Okay, You're Not

The Power Of Positive Thinking And How To Apply It When Your Mobile Phone Bill Comes In

---

Travel Tip

Happiness isn't a destination – unless, of course, you're on the way to the shoe sales.

THANK GOD YOU'RE NOT A SCORPIO

The Worst-Behaved Girls In The Universe

You don't need to look through a telescope or dress like a gypsy's poor relation in order to accurately predict that all men are bastards. You just have to know their star signs. From weak-as-water Pisces and stick-in-the-mud Taurus, to lightweight-as-air Libra and they-discovered-fire-about-the-same-time-as-they-discovered-me Aries, men can be defined and derided by dint of their astrological assignation.

But what about the women? I psychically hear you cry. If men are born congenital idiots, then surely girls sharing similar birthdays have similar traits? Sure they do. But what is seen as an embarrassing defect in one gender is often something to be applauded in the other. For instance, while a Pisces man will be ridiculed for blubbing constantly in public, a tearful Pisces girl will be praised for managing to look endearing and convincing as well.

Anyway, enough about the Pisces male. Let's talk about something more worthy and more interesting, like the worst-behaved girls this side of the galaxy.

The Aries Girl

You're as tough as old boots which is a good thing to be if you're wearing a pair and kicking a man while he's down. Wimps and weeds make you want to scream. Procrastinators and equivocators make you want to tear out their hair. And a bloke who pleads with you to stop wiping your boots on him and start acting more like a grateful female deserves to be treated like the doormat instead.

The Taurus Girl

Your best point is your ability to suffer fools. This, at first glance, might seem to make you easy pickings for complacent studs masquerading as unsightly couch potatoes or born-again commitment-phobes posing as eternal romantics. However, we said you were patient, not stupid. Any man dumb enough to take you for granted – or to take off without you – usually gets to experience your second-best point: your ability to nag and hound a person to death.

The Gemini Girl

Blessed with more personalities than a TV awards ceremony, you're an expert at massaging truths, manipulating men and beating the hell out of everyone when you're playing charades. Unkinder men will accuse you of being deceitful, fickle and ever-so-slightly mad. You'll no doubt reply by spinning your head 360 degrees and snarling that it's a demon seed's perogative to change its mind about what book/film/play it means to act out.

The Cancer Girl

You probably get the worst deal in the entire zodiac. Not only are you meant to like children and animals, you're also supposed to be a good cook. Therefore it's not surprising that you're also renowned for pitch-black moods and extremely long sulks. After all, a Cancer bloke only has to pour hot water over a pot of noodles to live up to his image of natural-born homemaker. You, on the other hand, have to remember to take the lid off as well.

The Leo Girl

It's very annoying being a beautiful, talented, intelligent show-off. Every time you so much as hint at how brilliant you are in bed, a man will say "I bet you're a Leo". If you even dare to suggest you know better than him when it comes to things like locating your G-spot he'll mutter "Typical bloody Leo". Of course, you could pretend to be modest and shy but then you'd never have an orgasm, would you?

The Virgo Girl

Being a dark horse does have its advantages. For one thing, the stable-hand doesn't have to clean you so often. Secondly, you can perpetuate the astrological myth that you're a virgin simply by refusing to reveal that you're not. Indeed, no man need ever know about your sordid past and your muddied mind so long as you keep your mouth shut and look like you think pure thoughts. (Men are so gullible that all you need, to do that well, is to wear a pair of white knickers.)

The Libra Girl

Your fair-minded ways and even-handed manner serve you well when it comes to dealing with the reprobate ways of the opposite sex. They screw around, so you screw around. They don't like doing the dishes, then neither do you. They want to watch sports on telly. Well, blow me down, it's your favourite pass-time too. Before too long, they'll be begging for you to nag, moan and tell them off like normal girlfriends do. Anything but be so goddamned reasonable and level-headed all the time.

The Scorpio Girl

It's a real drag being a Scorpio girl. Upon discovering your star sign, men have a habit of closing their eyes, crossing themselves, tossing salt over their shoulder and then expect you to deliver sex on tap. Don't they realize that saying *Hail Mary* doesn't count as foreplay? And, since they can't even be bothered to get your name right, they deserve to be tied to the bedposts and whipped. As for the salt you've had to pick up off your nice clean bedroom floor, well, what's a couple of nice open wounds for?

The Sagittarius Girl

Ever the optimist, you'll prefer to ditch a relationship rather than fix it because you just *know* there's a less crap one around the corner. This pragmatically romantic approach often incites accusations of flightiness from the losers you leave behind. They can do whatever they like so long as they don't start yelling and screaming and being negative in general while you're trying to get passionate with the newest love-of-your-life.

The Capricorn Girl

Pass on the paupers. Forget about romancing the proles. Money, power and status means more to you than anything else in the world, which in turn means you'll probably end up marrying a prince, a politician or a pop star, which in turn means you'll probably die from terminal boredom. Of course, you could forsake fame and fortune and try marrying for love instead but, trust me, you'll end up dying from terminal boredom anyway.

The Aquarius Girl

You look at men the same way scientists look at specimens on slides under microscopes. Unusual, yes, interesting, maybe, but certainly no cure for cancer. Men get upset when you treat them like objects, especially when you refuse to have sex with them either. And even if you do deign to shag them, they'll resent being used for experiments to test whether they are better in bed than a good book. Well, you're hardly going to shag the laboratory rat are you? Not after it's already knocked you back; twice.

The Pisces Girl

With your sweet, girlish charms obscuring a steely resolve, men only realize you're a bit like a bag of chocolate-covered bolts when they find themselves carrying you up and down sand dunes. Yes, you're scared of mice, but only when you don't have a hammer at hand. Yes, you can giggle at a man's joke, though only because you don't actually get it. And sure, you like long, romantic moonlit strolls on the beach, providing he doesn't expect you to walk.

Did You Know?

"What's your star sign?" is the most cringingly obvious chat-up line in the entire known universe.

PUT THE TOILET SEAT DOWN OR ELSE

D-I-Y Feng Shui

Don't waste valuable money hiring so-called experts to rearrange your furniture and fill your home with good karma. You don't need somebody else to tell you that if you boot your boyfriend out of the house, all your frustrations will disappear out of the door with him. After all, Feng Shui is less about ancient interior decorating techniques and more about good old common sense.

- Face your chair away from any windows so you aren't reminded that they need cleaning.
- Remove all mirrors to encourage feelings of self-esteem.
- Leave your front door unlocked so lovers don't feel trapped.
- Remove all kitchen fittings and appliances to avoid unnecessary guilt when eating take-away seven nights a week.
- Put a lock on your drinks cabinet to ward off greedy, grabbing house-guests.
- Put a can of air freshener in each room to ward off evil smells.
- Replace lights with candles to ward off evil electricity bills.
- Using numerology as a guide, change the number on your front door and really piss off the postman.
- Enhance your home's prosperity factor by getting rid of your telephone.
- Protect your home from unwelcome visitors by installing a burglar alarm.
- Increase luck by turning off irons, hair dryers and boiling saucepans before leaving the house.
- Create good vibes in your home by binning any album featuring Bryan Adams, Michael Bolton or Mariah Carey.

> **Caring Advice**
> *You can enhance the good fortunes of all the houses in your street simply by moving out.*

I CAN'T AFFORD TO SMELL THE ROSES

Aromatherapy On Less Than £10 A Day

You can spend an awful lot of money these days just to make your home smell of basil and juniper and geranium and rose. While aromatherapists sniffily claim that essential oils are essential for improving your state of mind as well, you can counter-claim that you'd feel happier and be a lot richer if you just moved out of the house and started living in the garden. However, since you probably like hoeing, pruning and weeding even less than vacuuming, stay indoors and use the scent of cheaper, more common household odours to wake up in a better mood.

Invigorating scents
- Shoe polish.
- Oven cleaner.
- Glue.

Stress relievers
- Freshly-brewed coffee.
- Cigarette smoke.
- Alcohol fumes.

Relaxants

- Lighter fluid.
- Leaking gas heaters.
- Smoke-filled rooms.

Aphrodisiacs

- New, crisp notes of any denomination (preferably in wads).
- Petrol fumes from a new sports convertible.
- Expensive after-shave.

Gentle Reminder

Rather than use reflexology techniques such as massaging your foot to conquer a pain elsewhere, why not just kick him instead?

I KNEW YOU'D DO THAT

Abusing Your Psychic Powers

Psychic power is a rare and special gift. Don't exhaust it helping policemen to pin-point the exact location of a corpse that's lying face down in the lower marshes of a tool shed on the southern-most tip of a reindeer's hoof. Use your supernatural insights to work out the more blindingly obvious instead.

- The phone rings far too early on Saturday or Sunday morning and you see visions of your mother at the other end of the line before even picking up the receiver.

- The phone rings in the middle of the night and you instinctively guess it's a friend calling from a different time zone.
- The phone doesn't ring and you innately know it's the man you met recently plucking up the courage to call.
- The second you step into the bath or outside your front door, having locked and bolted it and set the alarm, you intuitively feel that the phone will ring.
- The answering machine contains several messages which you correctly guess will be from people you don't want to hear from.
- Someone passes you an open box of chocolates; and you accurately predict that the good ones will already have been taken.
- Your friend falls madly in love and your gut tells you that this state of bliss will end in exactly three months.
- You know that the moment you light a cigarette is the moment that your bus/train/cab will arrive.
- You know that if you buy house/car/medical insurance you won't need it but also know that if you don't buy it, you will.

Stern Lecture
If you find activities like yoga and t'ai chi so exciting that you often get nose bleeds, it may be time to get a life.

KARMA IN A CAULDRON

An Advanced Course In Witchcraft

Witches get a bad rap. Whether it's the misunderstood old dears in *Macbeth* or the wicked one of the East that gave Dorothy's goody-two-ruby-shoes a run for their money, witches all get written off as battle-axes on broomsticks. Well, now is the time to enlighten the illiterate masses and show them that today's pagan goddesses come in all shapes and sizes – and not one of them carries a cleaning appliance.

Sex Curse Travel the world for unearthly sex, find a burst condom at the end of it, then say "Damn, bugger, bollocks, shit and hell" for as long as you like until the pregnancy results come through.

Love Curse Take a new-born babe, a nappy, a pin and a sprinkle of talcum powder, then present it at the altar of the proud father and tell him it's not his.

Career Curse Gather seven toadstools, the eyeballs of a newt, the spleen of a pig and the severed head of a decomposing goat you found behind a playground fence and throw them at your boss when you get into work.

Money Curse Walk into a bank manager's office, wave your bank charges statement three times in front of his nose and say: "May the arse of the black-hooded corporate tax beast and his five deaf, blind, dumb, illegitimate auditors chase you so far down the Valley of Doom that all your bank tellers will go on strike".

Health Curse Sit in a graveyard, smoke 60 foul and heady non-filtered cigarettes, drink the blood of 20 vodka and tomato juices, consume an entire box of Black Magic and wonder out aloud why you're not dead too.

Confucius Says
Girl with glass eye should never trust iridologist.

GOD IS GOOD, PASS IT ON

Catholicism And Other Crackpot Religions

Some girls believe that there's no such thing as God because if there were She wouldn't have invented thrush. Other girls only start believing in a divine entity when they're about to die from lack of sex caused by thrush. Despite your misgivings, it would pay you to realize that happy-clappy claptrap can play an important part in your quest for peace of mind.

Just think, so long as you believe, you can lie, cheat, steal, embezzle, or deliberately pass on fungal diseases to unwitting partners content in the knowledge that you'll still go to heaven after he's killed you.

Catholic

The pros: You can blame your bad figure on the 15 children you've had in swift succession.

The cons: You can't, while heavily pregnant, sit in a hot bath drinking gin while holding a pair of knitting needles, without people jumping to the wrong conclusion.

Buddhist

The pros: You might come back as a man-eating shark.

The cons: You might come back as a dolphin.

Muslim

The pros: You don't have to read *The Satanic Verses*.

The cons: You have to pretend that you respect men.

Hare Krishna

The pros: You can eat lentils and feel virtuous rather than poor.

The cons: Everyone expects you to sing *that* George Harrison song on karaoke nights.

Scientologist

The pros: You have to be extremely stupid, well-off or famous to join.

The cons: You have to read daft science-fiction books and take them as gospel.

Moonie

The pros: Your wedding is organized for you.

The cons: Your bridegroom is also arranged for you.

Mormon

The pros: You don't have to sleep with your husband every night of the week.

The cons: You have to pretend to like everything ever recorded by The Osmonds.

Orthodox Jew

The pros: You're part of an extremely close-knit community.

The cons: You have to marry another Orthodox Jew.

Jehovah's Witness

The pros: You learn very early on in life how to accept rejection.

The cons: People set their dogs on to you.

Born-Again Christian

The pros: You can unsettle heathens just by looking at them with your mad, staring eyes.

The cons: Everybody suspects you were an old soak and a wanton floozy in your former life.

Words of Praise

Embracing religion to any degree is to be applauded, even if it is as small as you putting your hands together and praying to God that no-one ever finds out you used to fancy Rod Stewart.

CAN'T YOU PUSH YOUR OWN SODDING WHEELCHAIR?

Struggling To Be A Saint For A Day

Use the daily checklist on the right to see whether acting pure of heart is better than being bad to the bone. Find out if the good karma you create around you is returned threefold. And see if you're actually capable of being generous, patient, kind, chaste, thoughtful and unselfish for a whole 24 hours.

- ❏ Tip cab drivers.
- ❏ Smile at complete strangers.
- ❏ Give money to every homeless person/charity collector/sponging sibling who asks for some.
- ❏ Arrive at all work appointments and social engagements on time.
- ❏ Give friends and acquaintances alike at least one compliment each per day.
- ❏ Say "yes" to every favour or imposition asked of you by colleagues or bosses.
- ❏ Eat only good and natural wholefoods.
- ❏ Refuse to frown at the girl behind the lunch bar when she says she's run out of white bread.
- ❏ Refrain from getting uppity with bank tellers and shop assistants.
- ❏ Reach out and helping little old ladies get the groceries they need from the top shelf in supermarkets.
- ❏ Allow shoppers with less items than you go before you in a super-market queue.
- ❏ Listen sympathetically to the problems of your friends without yawning too loudly.
- ❏ Refuse to burden your friends with your own more exciting problems.
- ❏ Enjoy an alcohol-free night out at your local pub.
- ❏ Refrain from snapping at the barman when he asks you what's wrong with you.
- ❏ Refrain from getting lecherous and flirting with married men.
- ❏ Ring your parents when you say you will.
- ❏ Go to church.
- ❏ Join the Samaritans.
- ❏ Become a Prison Visitor.
- ❏ Volunteer at a refuge.
- ❏ Foster a child.
- ❏ Adopt a Third World elephant.

❑ Take a "Nodding Heads and Smiling A Lot" course run by some fruit-loop, American, new-age guru.

__ **Total No. of Good Deeds Done**
__ **Total No. of Positive Responses From Recipients**
__ **Total No. of Negative Feelings Felt By Me**

Dark Thought

A bad girl is more likely to do someone a good turn if the man she fancies is close at hand to witness it.

Signs you might be ready for sainthood

- People have attempted to burn me at the stake.
- I occasionally get holes in the palms of my hands or the soles of my feet.
- I often hear the voice of God calling me.
- I often see visions of Mother Mary.
- I have a beatific smile.
- I am still a virgin.
- But I've got a son called Jesus.
- I haven't got any sons called Trevor.
- I prefer to wear sandals rather than trendy sports shoes.
- I prefer attending to the needs of the sick, the dying and the poverty-stricken, to going shopping.
- The Pope's got my private telephone number.
- I have been dead now for at least five years*.

* Minimum time spent dead before being considered for canonization.

GOD, I'M WONDERFUL

Affirmations For The Delusional

I think, therefore I am definitely female.

*I am a young, beautiful, rich, successful and intelligent female,
but I guess I can't have it all.*

*Feeling smug and self-righteous is much better than feeling like
a piece of cow dung.*

*If I get any more confident, I suspect I am going to become a
complete pain in the arse to be around.*

*Of course, the only reason I don't have any friends is because
they're all jealous of my newfound munificence.*

*And the only reason I can't get on with men is because they feel
threatened by my recently-discovered sense of superiority.*

*In fact, the only reason I have had so many disastrous relationships
is because all men are emotional cripples who don't read books,
let alone ones about positive thinking.*

*Anyway, it's better to have loved and lost than to have married
the pigs.*

Kindly Thought

*If telling yourself you're a wonderful human being doesn't come
naturally or sound particularly convincing, why not get a good
friend to lie and say it on your behalf?*

IT WASN'T IIKE THAT IN MY DAY

Mischief-Making Beyond The Millennium

And now, as the end draws nigh, it's time for a bit of wishful thinking. Without further ado, here's a fingers-crossed, let's-hope-it-happens forecast of behavioural trends and sorely-missed inventions that might take place well after the Year 2000.

Raccooning Like cocooning only completely different. A style statement made by girls who walk proudly during daylight hours still wearing the make-up they put on the night before.

Girlism Extreme political stance that encourages girls to get their own way and get on in life just by behaving like girls.

The New Improved Man Term used to define a man who acts just like a man always has done and always will do, and who has the grace and humility to apologize for doing so.

Virtual Pregnancies For the seriously unimpressed.

Disposable Knickers For bad girls with busy lives.

The Clayton's Condom For bad girls who don't like the smell, look, touch or feel of traditional condoms.

Stringless Tampons For bad girls who like to wander naked around the house with dignity.

Ride-On Vacuum Cleaners For obvious reasons.

Self-Cleaning Ovens Ditto.

Self-Assembling Furniture Furniture that assembles itself.

Low-Calorie Wine Fairly self-explanatory.

Table Evaporators Devices which instantly zap spilled wine.

Lighter Alarms Disposable lighters that emit ear-piercing shrieks whenever they end up in someone else's pocket or handbag.

Selective Hearing Phones Will only ring after ten o'clock in the morning and even then, only when the person at the other end of the line is someone you actually wish to speak to.

Sex-Change Operation Reversals Ideal after you realize that being a man isn't all it's cracked out to be.

Wise Words

Bad girls don't need guns – they can wound well enough with their tongues.

GET DOWN ON YOUR KNEES AND STAY THERE

Why Bad Girls Will Always Rule The World

We can make grown men cry.

We can have a laugh at our own expense.

We can sue a man for half his house.

We can make him sign a pre-nup.

We can go down in history.

We can go down on anyone we like.

We can celebrate being celibate.

We can have sex all the time.

We can have sex without having babies.

We can have babies without having sex.

We can have men's babies then raise them alone.

We can have more than one orgasm at a time.

We can fake them when we're tired.
We can blame all our shortcomings on PMT.
We can blame all the world's misery on men.
We can wear skirts and dresses and look sexy rather than silly.
We can wear the pants in a household.
We can take all our clothes off and look better than men.
We can take all our clothes off and get paid more than men.
We can strike for better wages everywhere else.
We can talk to the press.
We can fight our own battles.
We can beat up bullies and kick out cowards.
We can yell and scream louder than anybody.
We can sleep like a baby as well.
We can change our own light bulbs without expecting a standing ovation.
We can deliver a child into this world without expecting thanks.
We can remember people's birthdays.
We can conveniently forget our own.
We can drink ourselves under the table and still get up the next day.
We can feel like death and not complain.
We can break all our resolutions.
We can break every man's heart.
We can fall in love with a thousand lovers.
We can hate only one.
We can smoke like it's going out of fashion.
We can burn all our bras as well.
We can chain ourselves to railings.
We can lie in front of bulldozers.
We can stand before our kids.
We can stand behind our man.
We can stand up for our rights.
We can sit down for a pee.